1-12-00

# CyberAssistant

# CyberAssistant

**How to Use the
Internet to Get More
Done in Less Time**

D. A. Smith-Hemphill, Ph. D.

## AMACOM

American Management Association

New York ■ Atlanta ■ Boston ■ Chicago ■ Kansas City ■ San Francisco ■ Washington, D.C.
Brussels ■ Mexico City ■ Tokyo ■ Toronto

Special discounts on bulk quantities of AMACOM books
are available to corporations, professional associations,
and other organizations. For details, contact Special Sales
Department, AMACOM, an imprint of AMA Publications,
a division of American Management Association, 1601
Broadway, New York, NY 10019
Tel.: 212-903-8316 Fax: 212-903-8083

Library of Congress Cataloging-in-Publication Data

Smith-Hemphill, D.A.
    CyberAssistant : how to use the Internet to get more done in less
time / D.A. Smith-Hemphill
        p.     cm.
    Includes index
    ISBN 0-8144-7011-4
    1. Internet (Computer network)    2. World Wide Web
(Information retrieval system)    I. Title.
    TK5105.875.I57S62    1999
    025.04—dc21                                                    99–25848
                                                                        CIP

Printing number
10 9 8 7 6 5 4 3 2 1

To my husband, David. The best part about writing a book is being able to dedicate it to you.

# Contents

# **Acknowledgments**

To say thank you pays little compliment to the support and encouragement of my friends and family. So many people cheered me on that I would need another book just to list their names.

My clients provided valuable contributions by way of stories and anecdotes. I greatly appreciate having had the opportunity to work with and learn from such wonderful, generous people.

A special note of appreciation goes to my colleague Pat Nickerson, who was always a ready and enthusiastic counsel.

# Introduction: A Day in the Life

Picture this: It's Monday morning. You arrive at the office well rested from your weekend off, planning for the day at hand. You sit down at your desk ready to begin a well-organized, productive, nonchaotic day. However, the boss has a different plan for you. The first words you hear are, "I'm so glad you're here," and within the space of ten minutes the boss has made the following requests:

"Get me information on . . . "

"Book my trip to . . ."

"Find the specs on our competitor's product."

"Where's that package?"

"There's an article in the *Times* I need to see."

"I need directions and a map to . . ."

"Get theater tickets for me and my client the night of . . ."

"Find out what our customers are saying about our new product."

"Send this supplier an e-mail. What's its address?"

"Get a copy of the newest software upgrade for . . ."

You can feel your blood pressure rising, the knot forming in your stomach, and all you can think is, "How am I going to get all this done in addition to the work I had already planned to do?"

Wouldn't it be great to have your own assistant? Now you do. This book is designed to help you understand how to use the Internet as your assistant. You'll learn what it can do for you and how to use it as a tool to make your job easier.

Just think of what a good assistant could do for you, how much time and effort you could save. You spend hours:

- Making meeting arrangements

- Assembling travel options and prices

- Collecting information on products and services

- Seeking out and booking conference locations

- Researching background information for presentations

- Purchasing business supplies

Now you can assign those jobs to the Net and let those resources work for you.

Many people think of the Internet as a place to go to purchase items, to send and receive e-mail, to do research, or just to have fun. In fact, the Internet is great for all those things. Don't think of the Internet as having only one function. Think of the Internet as a multifunctional tool, your right hand, so to speak. The question to ask yourself is not "Should I use the Net?" but "How can I use the Net for researching, purchasing, information gathering, planning, scheduling, or other work I have to get done?" Let the Internet be your assistant. Let us show you how.

# Chapter 1

# Meet Your New Assistant

You may be wondering why the history of the Internet would be important to you. If you were hiring a human assistant, wouldn't you want to meet and interview that person? Wouldn't you have an interest in how past experiences have prepared him or her for the tasks at hand? The same applies to the Internet. The way in which the Internet has evolved affects how it can perform for you and contribute to your success.

Come meet your new assistant and see:

- How the Internet began

- Who uses the Internet

- How information travels over the global network

- The attraction of the World Wide Web

- The language of the Web—HTML

- Who's in charge of the Internet

## In the Beginning . . .

The Internet was never designed to be used as it is today. The birth of the Internet took place under the auspices of the U.S. Department of Defense. In the early 1970s, the Advanced Research Project Agency (ARPA) was charged with building an information transport network. Known as ARPANET, the goal of this system was to allow different computer systems to share information. It had to be a reliable transport system with no central hub. ARPANET was primarily to be used for linking military sites and was designed so that if one part of the network was destroyed, information could still be transferred and the network could continue to function. The early growth and development of what we know as the Internet took place primarily in government, as well as in research facilities and educational institutions.

For years, you transferred information by typing in strings of commands on a monochrome screen. There were no colors, no graphics, no point-and-click navigational tools to make it easy to find resources, just line after line of command code and text. You had to know the programming codes and commands because there was no graphical user interface. There was also very little danger of enjoying yourself or dramatically increasing your productivity.

Mosaic was the first graphical browser available. It was developed for navigating the World Wide Web by the National Center for Supercomputing Applications. Mosaic changed how we could interface with and transfer information by giving access to nonprogrammers, and the sky was the limit.

## Present Day

Today, all that has changed. You can "point and click" your way across cyberspace without ever typing a line of code. You see pictures and color. A multitude of tools are available to help navigate and find whatever you need. The Internet serves as one large trading post where anyone can offer or gather information. The U.S. Department of Commerce estimates that Internet traffic is doubling every 100 days.

The population of the Internet has changed as well. In the past, it was primarily scientists, researchers, and programmers. Chances are today that every company you do business with has a presence on the Net. The U.S. Department of Commerce states that electronic commerce on the Internet is estimated to reach $300 billion by the year 2002.

## Who Is on the Internet?

In answer to the question "Who uses the Internet?" it would be easier to figure out who is not using it than who is. You will find major corporations, small businesses, not-for-profit organizations, governments (U.S. and foreign), libraries, universities, associations, museums, the media, entertainment groups, individuals. Almost anything and anyone else you can imagine is on the Internet.

Various estimates tell us that anywhere from 45 million to 100 million people are now online. Since no one really controls the Internet, there is no accurate way to measure how fast it is growing. We do know that sites appear and disappear every day. As you can imagine, chaos prevails. The Internet was never designed or built as a cohesive system; it just happened, and continues to happen, much like the state of a teenager's room. No one quite knows how it got like this.

## How Does Information Travel Over the Global Network?

The structure of the Internet is made up of large and small computer networks, as well as individual computers that all use a standardized protocol (i.e., method of communication) to transfer information. Whether the computers are the same make or run the same operating system doesn't matter; they can still exchange information using this protocol.

Here's how it works:

The Internet has been described as a network of networks. A network is defined as two or more computers that are connected and can speak the same language to exchange information. If a network is "on the Net," then one of the computers in the network is called a server computer (see Figure 1-1). That server computer is assigned an Internet Protocol (IP) address. The address is a series of numbers that look like this:

---

### 203.176.56.193

---

This is called a **dotted quad format**. At present, none of the numbers in the address can be above 255. You may have seen a similar string of numbers at the bottom of your browser screen as you are searching, but for the most part they are invisible to us.

What we interface with is the Domain Naming System (DNS) that translates those numbers into names (i.e., microsoft.com). Names are much easier to deal with and remember than number strings. The address identifies that server computer to others in the system.

When you send a message, it goes to the computer that is providing your connection to the Internet. Your company may have its own computer "on the Net," which means that the computer has an IP address. Or you may be dialing into a service provider whose computer is on the Net and is charging you for the connection. Your message is divided into small units called packets, and each packet is "wrapped" with the destination address

**Figure 1-1.** The Internet is a network of networks.

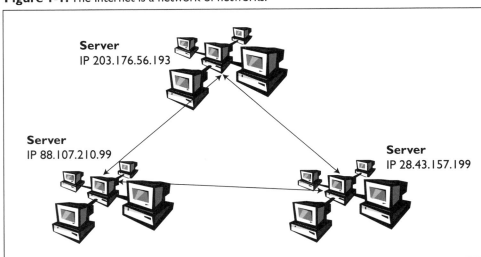

and information about how to reassemble the packets back into the complete message, in the right order, when they arrive at the destination (see Figure 1-2).

Each packet is then transmitted separately. You may have seen references to the abbreviation TCP/IP, which stands for Transmission Control Protocol/ Internet Protocol. TCP/IP forms the gift wrapping around each packet of information, and it represents the common language spoken by computers on the Internet. TCP carries the assembly information; IP, the destination address.

Once a message has been created, divided into packets, and gift wrapped, the transmitting computer looks to see if it has sent a message to that destination before and, if so, by what route. The route is established and the packets are sent by bouncing them from one computer to another. Parts of a single message might travel through computers owned by many different corporations, schools, libraries, associations, and government entities.

You may be wondering why you need to know this level of detail about how information travels over the Internet. To actually exchange information, you don't. All of this protocol business is transparent to the user. But you will be able to better understand certain error messages

**Figure 1-2.** Your message is divided into packages (known as packets) and wrapped with the destination address.

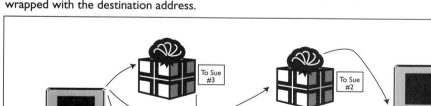

that are returned that mention TCP/IP. You'll impress your boss by being able to explain what the problem is when a message fails to go through, and knowledge is power!

It is also important that you understand the random way in which the Internet transfers information so that you are aware that the Internet is not foolproof; it is not entirely secure, private, or without its frustrations. The Internet is amazing, much like the human body, which transmits hundreds of thousands of nerve impulses. And because it is a complex system, there are many things that can go wrong as well.

## What in the World Is the World Wide Web?

You may think that the terms the *Internet* and the *World Wide Web* (WWW) are synonymous: Not true! The Web represents only a portion of the information on the Internet.

Like the Internet, the Web also started as an outgrowth of a research and academic project. The European Laboratory for Particle Physics (generally known as CERN) constructed a way of accessing information by using point-and-click technology instead of entering lines of code on the screen.

Think of the Web as a large group of filing cabinets with drawers full of documents. Imagine that you go to the cabinet, pull out a document, and start to read it. In the first sentence you see a word you need defined, so you put down the piece of paper and start to look around for a dictionary. When you find the dictionary, you open it, search for the word, and finally get the definition. These scientists were able to put a "tag" of text within your document so that when you got to that word, you could click on it and the dictionary would be brought to you, with the page open, and the correct definition highlighted.

## HTML: The Language of the Web

The Web is made up of documents that are connected by these tags. By using a Web browser, you see the tags as **hyperlinks** and make use of their connections. You can also see graphics, and that makes it much easier and more interesting. The tag contains all the commands to tell the system where to go and how to display the next set of information. From one document you can access any number of other documents that contain related information, without typing in any new addresses.

The Web is made up of millions of documents written in Hypertext Markup Language (HTML). This language allows the command-loaded tags to be embedded in the document so that all you see is text in boldface or underlined and usually in a different color, and all you have to do is click on that word or phrase. This text is the hyperlink, and when passing over that tag with your mouse cursor, the cursor changes to a hand-shaped icon. Clicking on the link tells the computer to find and load the website referred to by the HTML tag.

## What Can You Do on the Web?

The Web is primarily a place to get and give information. That may mean getting product information and giving payment, sending and receiving e-mail, or researching requests and results. You can offer information to others through a variety of channels: e-mail, your company website, newsgroups, discussion groups, and chat rooms. You can gather information by using search engines, surveys, newsgroups, and discussion groups. The Web is also a great place to shop for products and services at a growing number of commerce sites.

## Who's Minding the Store?

In short, the answer is, no one! The Internet is not owned or run by any-one. There are various agencies, however, that work hard to make sure the Internet serves you well. These include the Internet Society, the Internet Engineering Task Force, the W3 Organization, and the Internet Architecture Board. A company called Network Solutions, Inc. holds a contract to sell, register, and maintain Internet domain names that will expire in 2000; a changeover to a nonprofit registration body is already under way.

# Chapter 2

# Connecting With Your New Assistant

Getting connected to the Internet may be as easy as clicking an icon on your office computer's screen (see Figure 2-1). Your company has provided the hardware, software, and Internet connection. Just click and go!

**Figure 2-1.** When you see an Internet icon (such as the Microsoft Internet Explorer icon), you are a click away from being online.

If your office is the only place you'll be using the Internet and your computers are fully configured to allow you to connect from any location you choose, skip this chapter. If, however, you want to connect outside the office, or you need to help your boss get set up, read on. This chapter explains the hardware, software, and other components you will need to get started (see Figure 2-2).

**Figure 2-2.** The four components for connecting to the Internet.

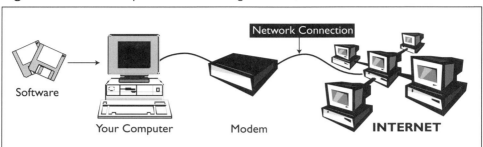

Please be advised that if your company isn't online yet, don't install anything yourself. The system administrator will want to control the process.

## The Physical Interface: Your Computer

The computer provides your physical interface with the Internet. You send information by typing in a designated text area and hitting a "send" or "submit" button. Then you read the reply on your computer screen.

Many people choose to use existing desktop or laptop machines and just add Internet functionality by installing special communications software. If you decide to buy new, the desktop and laptop machines for sale today come equipped with enough power to drive the necessary software. Many computers also come packaged with a modem and offers from service providers for trial periods with the necessary software preinstalled. New handheld computers that run the Windows CE 2.0 operating system are also capable of surfing the Net, and some models come with a built-in modem.

## Modems

The modem (short for modulator–demodulator) takes the digital signal generated from your computer and translates it into an analog signal so it can go out over telephone lines to the network connection on the Internet. When data come back to your computer over the phone line, the modem does the reverse translation, from analog to digital signal (see Figure 2-3).

**Figure 2-3.** The modem does modulation/demodulation, translating the signal from digital to analog and back again.

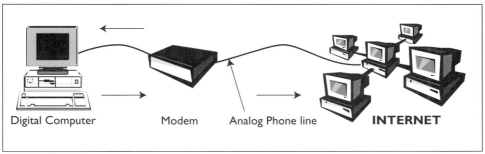

Digital Computer          Modem        Analog Phone line        **INTERNET**

Modems come in all shapes and sizes. For desktop computers there are both internal and external modems. The difference is whether or not you have to open the case of your computer to install the modem. If there is a place to plug in a standard phone line on your computer, you already have some kind of modem. You can buy modems the size of a thick credit card (known as a PC card) that fits in a slot in your laptop or handheld. In choosing a modem, there are two issues that are most important—speed and reliability. You want your connection to be both fast and reliable (i.e., so that it doesn't disconnect).

Modem speeds are measured in bits per second (bps), or the number of units of data that pass a certain point in one second of time. The fastest modems around are advertised as "56K" devices (56,000 bps).

Another option is an Integrated Services Digital Network (ISDN) adapter, which is a kind of digital modem. It takes the digital signal from your computer and allows you to communicate on a digital network. ISDN service may be available from your phone company, but it is more expensive. Using your TV cable system or a satellite hookup might also be an option in your area, and while you will get very fast transmission speeds, you will pay a premium price for it.

## Software

You'll need two types of software programs, one for connection and one for navigation. Connection software establishes the connection between your computer and the Internet-connected computer. This software dials the appropriate phone number and logs in with your user name and password. If you are accessing your office network, that number will be dialed; if you use a service provider, you will dial into its network instead. Then the connection software monitors the established communication link and facilitates data transfer. You will also need navigational software, e.g., a web browser, to take you where you want to go once you get to the Web. There's more about browsers in Chapter 3.

## Network Connection

In terms of a network connection, you have two basic choices: an Internet Service Provider (ISP) or an online service.

### Internet Service Providers

ISPs provide a gateway to the Internet and charge a fee to allow you to connect. Fees vary from provider to provider, but most provide monthly and hourly rates. The ISP lets you dial into its Internet-connected computer with your modem-equipped personal computer. Once connected, your computer can exchange data with any other computers that have an Internet address. Most ISPs will provide the software you need to make the initial connection to their service. That's the good news. The bad news is that while they provide these tools, they are aiming at a somewhat sophisticated user who knows how to (and wants to) configure and set up the system.

### Online Services

Online services focus on making the Internet more user-friendly. Services such as CompuServe, America Online (AOL), and Prodigy provide complete software packages with the connection options already configured. The goal is to make this process as painless and simple as possible. The process literally installs itself.

The only exception is for handhelds and palmtop machines. These end-user devices are not presently accommodated with the standard software called a dialing script from the online services. However, there are manual changes that can be made to allow you to use these machines on the Internet. Because of their small screens, handheld devices do not lend themselves well to "surfing the Net." They are useful, however, for handling e-mail messages while traveling and other basic functions.

Online services charge a fee comparable to that of an ISP, but that fee also includes access to subscriber-only content (e.g., bulletin boards, forums for specific interest groups, and chat areas).

## How Do I Choose Between an Online Service and an ISP?

As a general rule of thumb, online services are the best choice for beginners and folks who want an effortless setup and sign-on process. The four major services—AOL, CompuServe, Prodigy, and the Microsoft Network—offer free trial periods, so you can check out the service to see if it meets your needs. They also provide both national and international connection options if you are traveling. Traditionally, CompuServe has been thought of as the online service for business, but since AOL has acquired CompuServe, the delineation between the services is less clear.

ISPs provide more choices and options for experienced users who wish to have them or are willing to spend the time and energy to learn about and install different options. Some of the larger ISPs also offer trial periods and local city connections. The larger the ISP, the more likely it is to have twenty-four-hour technical support available to you on the phone and online.

If you have decided to use an online service, the best way to choose one is to get its software and make use of the trial period. Observe how the system is organized. Try not to be carried away with exciting graphics. Instead, evaluate any service according to such criteria as organization and content. Is it organized in a way to give you the kinds of information you want, or do you have to dig for information? Check out the internal content. Every service carries information such as news, weather, sports, and business topics. You will find forums, or newsgroups, for many business topics and vendors in which there is both broad and specialized interest. Make sure the "areas of interest" are of interest to you. Although my husband would appreciate access to the scores for the javelin-throwing contest last Thursday in Lower Slobovia, I don't want, need, or even like sports content. It doesn't help me do my job. Just between you and me, it doesn't help him do his job either; he just likes it.

## *Information to Know: Online Services*

**America Online (AOL)**
800-827-6364

**CompuServe**
800-848-8199

**Prodigy**
800-776-3449

**The Microsoft Network (MSN)**
800-373-3676

Choosing between ISPs doesn't involve content, because they don't offer more than what is on the Internet. The first decision here is between a local company and a nationwide one. The choice really relates to whether or not you want or need to access the Internet "from the road." If you are not going to take this show on the road, then a local ISP might be a little less expensive.

An ISP may charge for your initial sign-up, so be sure to ask. Also make sure that the ISP has a high reliability rating. If the ISP's Internet-connected computer is frequently out of service or overloaded, you have no access. Try dialing into the ISP's computer using your phone during the time frames when you would need access. If you hear the loud, screeching modem sound, it means you would be connecting to the service if you were using a modem and not just your phone. If you hear busy signals, look elsewhere for service. You will also want to know what software is included with the package, and if there is a charge. A complete listing of national and local ISPs can be found at **http://www.thelist.internet.com.**

## *Information to Know: ISPs*

**Netcom**
800-353-6600

**PSINet**
800-827-7482

**AT&T WorldNet Service**
800-967-5363

**EarthLink Network Inc.**
800-395-8425

## Questions to Ask: Choosing a Service Provider

Whether you are looking at online services or ISPs, the following categories of questions apply to both:

***Dialing charges.*** Is dialing into the service a local call, or will you have to incur toll charges for your online time? Those charges can add up. Do the services have local dial-in numbers for your travel destinations, national and international?

***Speed.*** What speed connection will the service accommodate? You may have a 56K bps modem, but if the service will only accommodate 28K bps speeds, then you will only be able to connect and transfer data at that slower speed.

***Help.*** Look at the online help screens and make sure they actually help you. Try calling the help line. (Making sure the service you are considering has a help line is the first hurdle. Making sure it's free is the second.) You will find this number included in the start-up package you receive or sometimes in the "About" topic on the Help drop-down menu. Don't use the line reserved for "new users" because it may not give you the true picture for ongoing support. Ask for the hours that support is available, and make sure that the times coincide with when you're likely to be online. Evaluate hold times and the quality of the assistance you get. If the support representative responds to your request with statements such as "That's a new one on me!" there's a clue.

***Additional charges.*** What are the monthly fees? Are you being charged a flat fee for unlimited usage? Are there timed usage charges (i.e., $2.95 per hour)? Are there any premium charges either for specific services or faster dial-in speeds?

***Services.*** Do the fees include e-mail service, e-mail attachments, newsgroups, discussion groups, FTP downloads, or a personal web page?

***Business record.*** How long has the service provider been in business? How often is its equipment updated? How many subscribers does it have? There may be a user's forum, so sign on during the trial period and see what existing customers of the service have to say.

***Word of mouth.*** Last but not least, ask around. Specific questions about how people use the service will help you learn more than simply asking if they like the service they use. If you ask, "Do you like your service provider?" most folks will reply yes, because they'd look ridiculous staying with a service they didn't like, and you have no more information than when you started. Think of the things that you want to accomplish or find on the Internet—research, news analysis, product or company information—and ask how the users of a particular service get the same information. Does the service appear to be fast and efficient, or cumbersome and a pain in the neck? This should give you some good comparative information with which to make your choice.

## A Word of Caution

The first time you connect you will use the ID and password provided for you by the vendor. Many services allow you to establish an ID of your choice. Once that is set up, it doesn't change. However, your password needs to be changed as soon as possible thereafter, and often. This is a security measure. A secret password should be just that, a secret. A good rule of thumb is to change your password monthly, and anytime you think it may not be a secret anymore. A secure password uses more than five characters, mixes upper and lower case letters, uses punctuation and numbers if allowed, and is not a word commonly found in the dictionary. Please don't use the same password every time you need a secret password (e.g., at the bank, video store, and for your luggage lock combination). If someone gets access to it, you'll be sorry. If you wish to write down your password, store it in a safe place such as your bank safety deposit box. A safe place does not mean written in your address book alongside the name of your service and the dial-in number. Enough said.

# Chapter 3

# Tools for Navigating the Net

In this chapter we take a look at your new assistant's resume. What tools does the Internet bring to the workplace? What skills and capabilities? Just as if you were hiring a person, you'll want to see what your new cyberassistant, the Internet, has to offer you to make your job easier.

In this chapter you'll learn about the tools available for navigating the Internet. We'll cover addressing, browsers, directories, search engines, newsgroups, discussion groups, and more.

Because more than 80 percent of the corporate market works on PC-based systems, the keyboard conventions for Macintosh computers are not included here. But Mac users, take heart! The same tools and techniques apply for you.

How do you find a needle in a haystack? A contact lens on the beach? Without the right tools and the right thought processes, finding usable information on the Internet is an equally impossible task. Luckily, there are some very useful tools available to you. This chapter will show you what tools you can use and how they work. Chapter 5 will tackle the actual search process.

## Addressing

The first thing to understand is addressing. There are two major types of addresses: e-mail addresses and Uniform or Universal Resource Locators (URLs).

## E-Mail Addresses

An e-mail address looks like this:

```
who@where.what
```

The address is made up of a "who" part, which identifies the user; the "at" symbol (**@**), which is used as a separator; and the "where.what" part, which is the domain name. The domain name is the name of the computer that houses this address. The address **Bob@aol.com** means that the message is put in Bob's message slot in the AOL computer. The domain name is separated into a lower ("where") and upper ("what") domain name separated by a dot. Though this is a period on your keyboard, it is referred to as a dot when used as a separator. The upper domain name (the "what" suffix) signifies the type of organization with which Bob is affiliated.

### *Common Suffixes*

**.com**   commercial organizations or corporations
           Example: FedEx
           **fedex.com**

**.gov**   government offices and agencies
           Example: The White House
           **whitehouse.gov**

**.edu**   educational centers, universities, and colleges
           Example: Massachusetts Institute of Technology
           **mit.edu**

**.org**    not-for-profit organizations
            Example: American Management Association
            **amanet.org**

**.mil**    military organizations
            United States Navy
            **usnavy.mil**

**.net**    pertaining to the Internet
            Example: Cybercraft
            **cybercraft.net**

You may also see a two-letter country code at the very end of the string—for example, **.uk** for United Kingdom or **.jp** for Japan. **Oxford.edu.uk** is, then, the address for Oxford University in the United Kingdom (**.uk**). Make sure you are precise when entering an address. To trick you into accessing their site instead, some people may use an address for their site that is similar to a more popular site.

### Sending an E-Mail Message

To send information to a person, you need only enter that person's e-mail address in the "to" section of your e-mail message. If you use an online service such as CompuServe and you are sending a message to someone outside the CompuServe network, you'll also need to add a heading to tell the system what kind of address it is—for example, **INTERNET:bob@aol.com** signifies that the message has to travel outside of CompuServe's system and across the Internet to reach Bob, who uses AOL. If you are on a corporate system and have trouble sending messages to folks outside your company, ask your system administrator for the heading you need to use.

## Uniform or Universal Resource Locators (URLs)

A URL is not a place to send mail. It is exactly what it says it is: the address of a resource or page of information you can access using browser software. In the literature, the terms *Universal* and *Uniform* appear to be interchangeable. I have included both so as not to confuse you.

A typical URL might look like this:

```
http://www.amanet.org
```

In a URL, the Hypertext Transfer Protocol (HTTP) is always the first part of a web address separated by a colon and double forward slash from the next part of the address (e.g., http://). The **http://** part of the URL in effect says, "Everyone speaking Hypertext Transfer Protocol listen up. Go to the World Wide Web, connect to this computer (amanet.org), and open the home page." Web addresses have no blank spaces in them and are not case sensitive. Two symbols—the hyphen (-) and the underscore ( _ )—can be used to delineate spaces.

The home page is the starting place or table of contents for the website (see Figure 3-1). The website represents all the linked documents to that home page, or the rest of the book pages documented in the table of contents. From the home page you could click on the link you want and go to that next document without having to know the address. So if you click on "United States" on the American Management Association (AMA) home page, you will find yourself at the Index page for the AMA in the United States (see Figure 3-2).

You may know the address of a specific document such as **http://www.amanet.org/xxx/yyy,** which says, "Go to this website and open this folder (**xxx**) and look at this document (**yyy**)." If you have the address of a resource, you are home free. It's a little like shopping. You know what it is you want and the store from which you want to buy. All you need is transportation.

## Browsers: Your Transportation

A browser is a graphical interface tool you use to access content on the Internet. A browser works like a taxicab. You tell it where you want to go (i.e., the address) and it takes you there. In the upper left corner of most browsers you will see a fill-in bar labeled Location or Address. You

**Figure 3-1.** American Management Association's home page is the starting place or table of contents for the website.

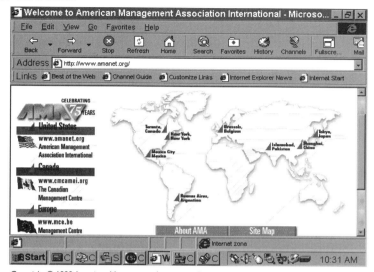

**Figure 3-2.** American Management Association's United States Index page is a specific document you can link to from the AMA's home page or by typing in the precise address for the document in the bar labeled Location or Address.

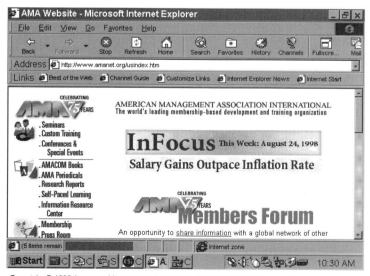

would type in the address in this box and away you go to that specific location.

Most browsers today don't require you to type the **http://** part of the address. Netscape Navigator allows you to type in just the computer name and the software automatically fills in the **http://www.** and the **.com** part of the address. If the address you wish to go to does not start with **http** and end with **.com**, type in the exact address you wish to access. The browser takes the address you supply and translates it to the IP address (e.g., 234.98.176.5) of the computer that houses the information you want to see. A copy of that page of information is presented on your screen, with all the linked information, or hyperlinks, shown in bold or underlined and usually in colored text (see Figure 3-3).

The power of the browser software is that it can "see" the hypertext tags embedded in the document pages you view. By clicking on any of these tags, the browser takes you to that next page. You don't have to tell a taxi driver which route to take, and you don't need to give the browser directions to take you to that linked page. Just click on the link and your request is carried out.

**Who Are the Players in Browser Software?**

In the marketplace today, the two primary browsers are Netscape Navigator and Microsoft Internet Explorer. Your corporate system will probably have one or the other loaded and ready for your use. They both work in primarily the same way and do primarily the same things.

For example, if you click on the Netscape logo at the top of the screen in Figure 3-5, that will take you to the Netscape home page. Microsoft's home page can be accessed in the same way, by clicking on the word "Microsoft" in Figure 3-4.

Each product has a window to display information, a scrollbar, and a status bar at the bottom of the window to show you what's happening

 **Make sure the address is entered correctly, or your request will go to the wrong place or to no place fast.**

**Figure 3-3.** Linked information, or hyperlinks, on a web page appear as either bold or under-lined text. Click on any hyperlink and you are carried to another page of information.

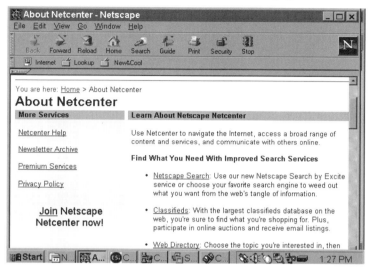

with your request. Each product uses distinct menu bars and buttons, as shown in Figures 3-4 and 3-5. Both Netscape Navigator and Microsoft Internet Explorer use a graphic in the upper right hand corner of the window, an "N" and "e," respectively, that rotates when information is being transferred or a request is taking place. They each have a Location or Address box that tells you the address of your current page. You can also access a history list of each web page address you have typed in by clicking the small arrow to the right of the Location or Address box. You can choose how many days' worth of history you wish to keep through the View/Internet Options settings in Microsoft Internet Explorer or through the Edit/Preferences settings in Netscape Navigator. Using the history list lets pages load faster because they are stored locally on your hard drive; the downside is that if you keep too many pages store in cache, you are wasting drive space.

**Figure 3-4.** The Microsoft Network home page as displayed in the Microsoft Internet Explorer browser window.

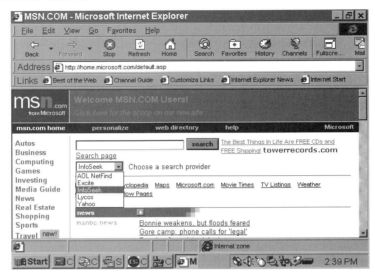

**Figure 3-5.** The Netscape Netcenter home page as displayed in the Netscape Navigator browser window.

By clicking on an address on the drop-down history list, the browser will take you directly back to that page. The Back and Forward keys move you a single page at a time in sequence through the pages you have accessed during the current session. There will also be a drop down box to show you how far back you can go. If you are using an IBM-compatible PC, you can substitute the keyboard shortcuts **Alt** ← (left arrow) for Back and **Alt** → (right arrow) for Forward.

If your computer stops in the middle of loading a web page on-screen, use the Refresh or Reload function to generate another request for the page that you want to see. Remember that information can take many different routes transferring along the Internet. By using the Reload/Refresh button, you are asking it to take a different route. The same repeat request is useful if you click on a hypertext link and nothing happens. Just click again and you should see progress.

Occasionally you may encounter messages such as "Server not responding" or "Server not found." The first thing to do is click the Reload/Refresh button on your browser to make another request for the information. If that doesn't work, then the server may be overloaded and you'll want to try again later.

The Stop button will do just that—actually stop the loading of a page altogether so you can skip to a different request. The Print function or button will print the page you have on-screen, and the Edit/Find function will bring up a small window to locate specified text on the currently loaded web page.

## How Effective Is My Browser?

The effectiveness of the browser isn't so much in the software itself, but in how you use the tool to organize your navigation of the Net.

If you use the same cab drivers over and over again, they will know the places you like to go. Browsers do the same thing. In Netscape Navigator this list of favorite websites is called Bookmarks; in Internet Explorer it is called Favorites. If you find a site that you know you'll want to visit on a regular basis, bookmark it or add it to your favorites list so you no longer have to remember the address. While you are at the website, click the Bookmark/Favorites command and select Add. Your favorite web page is now only two mouse clicks away. The two major browser makers also offer other tips for using their software at their websites. For Navigator tips, check out **www.netscape.com,** and for tips on using Internet Explorer, visit **www.microsoft.com.**

## Maintenance

Maintenance is important. Review your favorites list quarterly and clean out addresses on the list you no longer need. It's a little like taking out the garbage, but with much less lifting.

Organize your bookmarks into folders to combine individual site links into groups. That will make your bookmark/favorites list less cluttered and easier to navigate.

In Navigator, highlight the toolbar's Bookmarks icon. The Bookmarks drop-down menu will appear. Select Edit Bookmarks, then go to the File menu and choose New Folder (see Figure 3-6). In Internet Explorer, go to the Favorites menu and choose Organize Favorites. In the dialog box that appears, click on the New Folder icon (see Figure 3-7). In both programs, you can then drag and drop the bookmarks you want to reside in that folder. You can also have folders within folders to build a hierarchy.

You may have inherited a computer with a browser already installed that has someone else's bookmarks listed. If they did the same job that you will be doing, take the time to check their bookmarks carefully because they may have discovered some wonderful resources of which you are unaware and may want to keep. Then you can delete bookmarks that are of no use to you.

Unfortunately, I am a "just in case" saver, which means I bookmark almost everything just in case I might possibly need to refer to it again in my lifetime. That doesn't make for effective browser usage if my Favorites/Bookmarks list is three miles long. My solution is to keep a sep-

 **Make sure to use a database that is text-searchable so that you can use any of the entry text to find sites you have cataloged.**

**Figure 3-6.** Creating a new Bookmarks folder in Netscape Navigator is easy when you use the drop-down File menu.

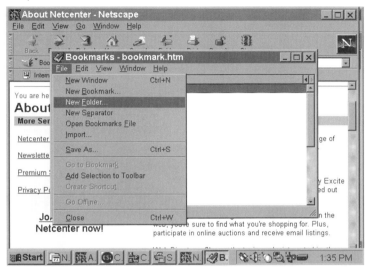

**Figure 3-7.** To organize your favorite web pages in Microsoft Internet Explorer, click the New Folder button in the Organize Favorites dialog box.

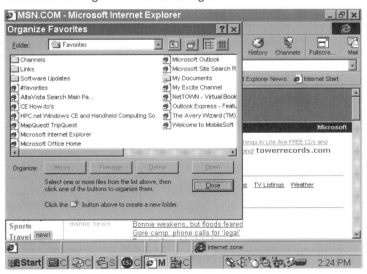

**Figure 3-8.** A simple database is a way to keep information about important but less frequently visited web pages—and it will keep your Favorites/Bookmarks list from becoming overly long and cluttered.

| Site Name | Site Address | Description | Who | Use when/with whom? |
|---|---|---|---|---|
| AMA | www.amanet.org | American Management Assoc. | Bob W. | Need research or training information |
| @Brint | www.brint.com | Business Researcher's Interests | Deb S. | Great research site for presentations and general business topics |
| | | | | |
| | | | | |
| | | | | |

arate database of those just-in-case addresses (see Figure 3-8) and to reserve my favorites list for sites I access at least twice a month or more. The database includes the site address, a description of the information available there, who referred me to that site, and how, when, and with whom I might use that particular website.

Another level of organization can be achieved by using bookmark categories to group bookmarks that are related to a specific topic (see Figure 3-9). Categories are very useful in organizing your bookmarks and keeping a history list that is usable. If you make a just-in-case category, you can keep those websites you really do access and get rid of others. Remember that it is also good practice to clear your history file on a regular basis so as not to use up precious disk space.

## Customizing Your Start Page

The start page is the first one to appear when you open your browser. You can customize this page to contain information you want to see. You might set it up so that your local weather five-day forecast, today's financial headlines, and your favorite travel site are on the screen (see Figure 3-10). You won't have to type in an address, just point and click on the icon for an area you want to access.

**Figure 3-9.** Organizing bookmarks by categories in Netscape Navigator is another way to find previously viewed web pages.

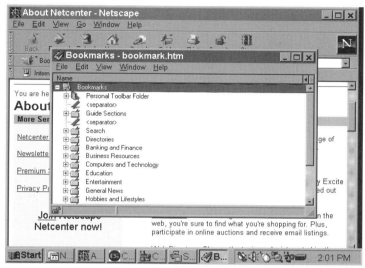

**Figure 3-10.** My personal start page includes local weather forecasts from Concord, CA and each day's top news stories.

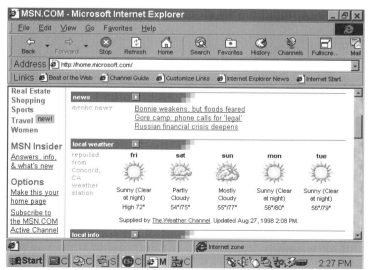

You can customize your start page to be any page address you specify, a blank page, or the place you left off when you finished browsing the last time. My sister hates to cook. She'll tell you that she only goes through the kitchen to get to the garage. If you find yourself only opening your browser so that you can go straight to your favorite site or search engine home page, then it makes sense to make that home page your start page.

To customize a start page in Internet Explorer 4.0:

1. Select the pull-down View menu.

2. Select Internet Options.

3. Click on the General tab in the Internet Options dialog box.

4. Type in the URL of the page you want to use as your home page in the Address field. You may also click on the Use Current button if you want to assign the current page to be the home page (see Figure 3-11).

In Netscape Navigator 4.0 (see Figure 3-12):

1. Select Preferences from the pull-down Edit menu.

2. Select Navigator in the category list on the left side of the dialog box.

3. Type in the URL of your desired home page in the Location field. If the page currently open on your screen is the one you want to use, click on Use Current Page.

Netscape has a nice feature that will let you use your bookmarks as your start page. Instead of putting in the URL, put in the location of the bookmark.htm file, usually **c:\Netscape\Defaults\Bookmark.htm**. The Browse button lets you find bookmark files stored on your hard drive in your computer's Netscape directory.

## Pushing and Shoving

A browser technology that can save you time and effort is "push" technology. If you know you'll need to see stock prices every hour throughout

**Figure 3-11.** Selecting a start page in Microsoft Internet Explorer is done through the View/Internet Options menu selection.

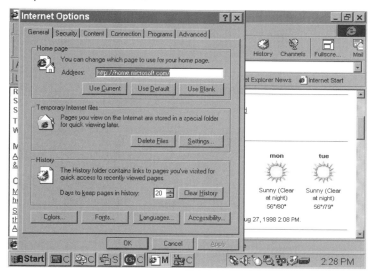

**Figure 3-12.** Selecting a start page in Netscape Navigator is done through the Edit/Preferences menu selection.

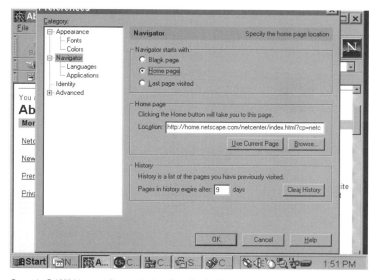

the day, push technology (also called webcasting) allows that information to be "pushed" to your computer rather than your having to go request it. The information is automatically sent to you. It arrives as e-mail, on your pager, or is downloaded to your computer using a schedule you define when you subscribe to the service. Some subscriptions require a fee; some are free. You can go to look at the information on the Web anytime that you want, because they are really just web pages. However, if you want the information pushed to you, you'll need to subscribe.

In Microsoft Explorer 4.0 you can display a channels bar on the side of your screen (see Figure 3-13) by clicking on the Channels icon at the top of the browser window. These "channels" represent nothing more than a graphical version of a favorites list and will connect you to channels from which you can make push requests. When the channel information is updated, an asterisk will appear in that channel bar. Some of the channels can even be used as screen savers. This technology works well for people who have an open connection to the Internet throughout the day. Your system administrator will tell you what kinds of push technology your setup and resources can handle.

### Push Strategy

How will you decide which information you want pushed to you? Your best strategy is to peruse the channels directory. Begin by downloading Microsoft's content list by clicking on the Channels guide. As you look at the selections, ask yourself:

- What information would I be requesting on a daily basis?

- Which information has the highest impact for me or for my boss?

- Does the information need to be real-time (i.e., news stories, stock prices)?

- Am I better off requesting the information as I need it, or does speedy, immediate delivery of new information matter more?

You can sign up directly from this screen if you choose, but beware. You are opening the gate for more data at your desk. Make sure any infor-mation you want pushed is of high value to you.

**Figure 3-13.** The Channels bar is a unique feature of Microsoft Internet Explorer that acts as a graphical version of a favorites list from which you can make "push" requests.

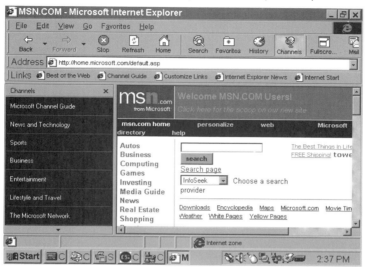

Inquisit provides a "personal business intelligence service" (see Figure 3-14). When you go to the Inquisit website, you specify what you are interested in knowing and Inquisit monitors its database of more than 600 information and news services. When an article fits your specifications, it is tagged for you. Updates are sent to you per the schedule you requested. This is also referred to as agent technology. Your software agent is doing the monitoring, tagging, and sending for you.

The PointCast Network provides an actual ticker scroll across the bottom of your screen with content from CNN, local newspapers, whatever you choose. The more specific you are in your request, the more these types of services can help you.

Take push technology one step further by using a notification service. If your boss is an investment banker and about to go into a presentation on a stock offering, you can keep him up-to-date on any changes in the stock price

**Figure 3-14.** The Inquisit home page lets you subscribe to a personal business intelligence service.

Reprinted with permission of Inquisit.

prior to the meeting. Let your Internet assistant do this by directing whatever "push service" you use to notify the boss's beeper when a significant change in price occurs.

### *Information to Know: Push Services*

Inquisit                          **www.inquisit.com**

The PointCast Network             **www.pointcast.com**

## Airport, Lady?

The people who design browser software understand the taxicab function of the software very well. If I come out of the front of the hotel with my suitcases and jump into a cab, the driver might ask, "Airport, lady?" The drive is antic-

**Figure 3-15.** A right-mouse click in any web page in Internet Explorer brings up a pop-up menu that you can use to create a desktop shortcut for that page.

Reprinted with permission of Inquisit.

ipating where I might want to go. Browsers do the same thing. The know one of the most common places you'll want to go is to search for information, so they have a search command that will take you to the major search engines. The Directory command performs a similar function by giving you access to online directories like Four 11 and Bigfoot. We'll talk more about these tools later in this chapter.

## Desktop Shortcuts

Another way to enhance the productivity of your browser is to create desktop shortcuts to your most used websites. Save this for the one or two sites you access the most during the day.

From Microsoft Internet Explorer or Netscape Navigator, right-mouse click in the page for which you want to create a shortcut and select Create Shortcut from the pop-up menu (see Figure 3-15).

**Figure 3-16,** To turn off images in Netscape Navigator, go to the Edit/Preferences dialog box and uncheck Automatically Load Images. It will save you download time.

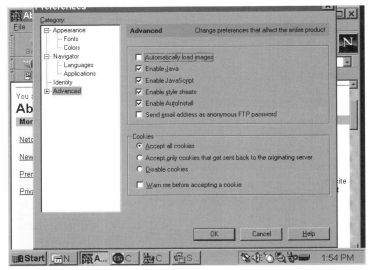

## When Speed Counts

To speed up the loading of web pages on your screen, turn off the graphics. Graphics are made up of millions of information bits and take longer to download to your machine than text. The pages won't look nearly as interesting or attractive, but they will appear on your screen much faster. You can turn graphics off through your browser for all sites or use the text only selection offered by some websites. In Navigator 4.0 (see Figure 3-16):

1. Go to the Edit menu.

2. Select Preferences.

3. Click on the Advanced category in the list on the left-hand side of the dialog box.

4. Uncheck or deselect Automatically Load Images.

To turn off images in Internet Explorer 4.0:

1. Select the View menu.

2. Select Internet Options.

3. Click on the Advanced tab in the dialog box.

4. Scroll down to the selections under the Multimedia category.

5. Uncheck or deselect the Show Pictures box.

## Directories

Directories work very much like the Yellow Pages. You select the topic you are interested in, and a list of relevant sites appears. Let's use a shopping analogy for a moment: You may know what you want to buy and the kind of store that might carry that item, but not the specific store you want to go to. You need to shop around. You might go to your Yellow Pages directory and look up that type of store—major department stores, for example. You choose a store from the list and note the address. When you arrive at the store, you look at the store directory to zero in on the department of the store that carries the item you want. When you get to that department, you locate the rack that carries your size. You'll try on the item, and you either buy it or go to the next store and repeat the process. The process starts with a broad category, and you keep "drilling down" until you zero in on your target. Directories work the same way.

### Choosing the Best Directory Tool

How do you know a good directory? Study the way it is set up. If it is organized in a way that allows you to find things quickly and easily, and it follows your logic thought pattern, then that tool is a good one for you.

We all know people whose desk looks as if a bomb just went off on it. You look at those desks and think, "How can they find anything in that mess?" Yet if you ask them for a document, they can produce it immediately. They have an organizational structure (i.e., a directory) in their head

**Figure 3-17.** The folks at Yahoo! have a sense of humor and know how to organize information exceptionally well on their home page.

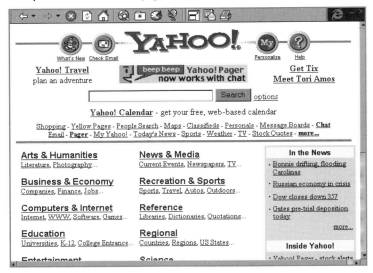

that they use to go straight to the information you requested. Different structures work better for different people. You need to find the tool that works best for you.

### *Yahoo for Yahoo!*

The largest and best known Internet directory is Yahoo! (**www.yahoo.com**). No, it doesn't stand for, "Yahoo, I finally found what I needed on the Internet!" It stands for Yet Another Hierarchical Officious Oracle. The Yahoo! folks have a sense of humor, and it shows on their site as well (see Figure 3-17). This site is an excellent business resource if you want to do broad to narrow concept searches.

Let's say you have just received a new assignment that involves coordinating travel. You'd like to know what resources might be out there for you, but you are looking for the big-picture view. From the main screen in Yahoo!

**Figure 3-18.** Selecting the Yahoo! Business and Economy directory lets you drill down to other specialized categories of information.

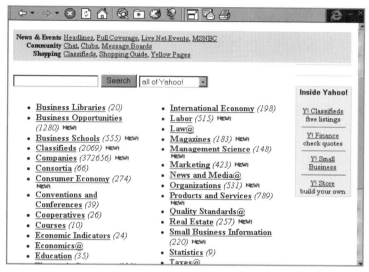

select the Business and Economy directory. Alternatively, you might select Travel from the Recreation and Sports directory. Since you aren't interested in tourist travel, however, the Business and Economy selection seems a better choice.

Once that set of categories appears (see Figure 3-18), you can type the word *Travel* in the search box and you will be rewarded with a list of additional categories that show you what is listed in the directory.

You will also be rewarded with an advertising banner, which you can choose to click on or bypass (see Figure 3-19). The bad news is that you have advertising on your screen, the good news is that the banner is chosen based on your area of interest, so you might find a valuable resource.

Many people find Yahoo! to be a favorite tool. When asked why, they say, "I can find the most information with it." What I think they mean is that Yahoo! can get them to information they can use faster than any other tool they have available.

Volume is not the key; relevance and value are. You could probably search the entire Web for business travel, but you'd have such a big list to go through you might never find the best or right resources for your specific need. The prescreened and organized quality of directories such as Yahoo! makes them invaluable.

The usefulness of any directory is based on how you rate the judgment of the people who built it. They decided what you would want to know about the subject area and how that information should be organized to meet your needs. Did they do a good job? Each directory approaches this information from a different angle, but they are all valid. For many users of the Internet, the information Yahoo! chooses and the way it is organized is of great value to them.

Most directories provide you with annotations or descriptions of other sites they include in their list. They tell you where the site is and evaluate or rank the quality of the content. For example, Windweaver (**www.windweaver. com/searchtools.htm**) provides reviews of many Internet search tools in annotated form. Figure 3-20 shows the information that appears on Windweaver about the AltaVista search engine.

### *Information to Know: Directories*

| | |
|---|---|
| Yahoo! | **www.yahoo.com** |
| Net Guide | **www.netguide.com** |
| Galaxy | **www.einet.net** |
| WebCrawler | **www.webcrawler.com** |
| Magellan | **www.magellan.excite.com** |
| Excite | **www.excite.com** |
| Windweaver | **www.windweaver.com** |

**Figure 3-19.** A Yahoo! search for the world "travel" brings up a list of category matches, as well as the ubiquitous advertising banners.

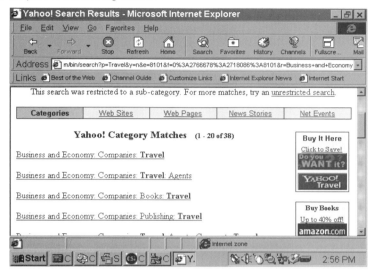

**Figure 3-20.** Windweaver is a directory that links you to different Internet search tools and reviews them in annotated form.

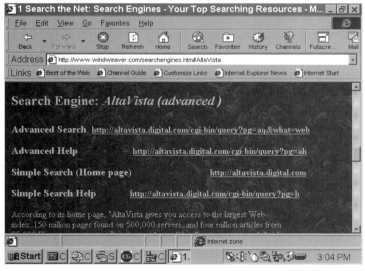

Reprinted with permission of Windweaver Training.

**Figure 3-21.** Bigfoot helps you track down people's e-mail or physical address.

Reprinted with permission of Bigfoot International Inc.

## People Find

Directories allow you to find not only information but people. Go to the site and type in whatever information you have—maybe a last name and a city—and let the directory do the legwork for you.

You can find e-mail addresses as well as street addresses and phone numbers. Some directories will even let you do a reverse search: Enter the

 **If you get a mystery e-mail and you can't tell who sent it by the return address, and no name was left, go to Bigfoot, an e-mail address search directory, and click Advanced Search (see Figure 3-21). Using Profile Search, type in the return address. Will wonders never cease!**

phone number and it returns the name and address. The directory will do its best to reward you with matches.

### Information to Know: Phone/Address Books on the Internet

| | |
|---|---|
| Big Yellow | **www.bigyellow.com** |
| Big Book | **www.bigbook.com** |
| Switchboard | **www.switchboard.com** |
| World Wide Yellow Pages | **www.yellow.com** |
| World Pages | **www.worldpages.com** |
| Infospace | **www.infospace.com** |
| The Ultimate White Pages | **www.theultimates.com/white/** |

### Information to Know: E-Mail Address Search Directories

| | |
|---|---|
| Four 11 | **www.four11.com** |
| WhoWhere | **www.whowhere.com** |
| Bigfoot | **www.bigfoot.com** |
| Internet Address Finder | **www.iaf.net** |

## Questions to Ask: Evaluating Directories

Here are some criteria for evaluating directories:

- What is the size of the database?

- How often is it updated?

- Is the organizational structure run by people or software?

- Does that structure make sense to me? Is it logical?

- Is there a search engine to allow keyword searches of the directory structure?

- Are the annotations helpful to me?

## Search Engines

Search engines differ from directories in the way in which they retrieve information. A search engine is made up of a large database that catalogs the content of web pages and an engine to search it. Depending on the database, it may catalog every word of text in a web page, just the concept, or an abstract of the page. The "engine" is really a piece of software that uses keywords you type in to produce matching results.

If we continue our shopping analogy one step further, search engines work like personal shoppers. You want to buy a birthday present for your dad, but you have no time to shop. You contact the personal shopper with your request—a man's red sweater, size large. The shopper will bring to you a variety of garments from which to choose. Your personal shopper doesn't haul you to the stores as the taxi (i.e., the browser) did, nor does your shopper make you do the work of finding a store and then zeroing in on a department as the directory did. A search engine, just like a personal shopper, brings what you're looking for to you.

With the browser you have to know the address. With a directory you need to know areas of information and you must have the big-picture view. Search engines are best suited to satisfying the need for a specific bit of information. You have to know exactly what you want. The more specific you can be, the more focused your results will be. If you ask for men's sweaters in medium-weight wool with a crew neckline, in fire-engine red, no trim, size large, you won't have to wade through fifty sweaters to get to the one you really want.

The name "search engine" would lead you to believe that when you make a request, the engine goes searching the Internet for what you want. But that's not the case. A search engine is really a large database into which Internet pages have been indexed. During off-hours the engine sends software robots called crawlers, wanderers, worms, or spiders out

**Figure 3-22.** AltaVista is a popular search engine among business professionals because of its full-text search capabilities.

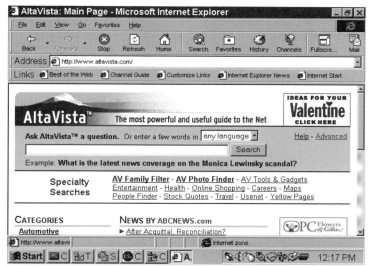

Reprinted with permission of Compaq Corporation.

on the Web to see what's new and bring it into the database. At the moment you make a request, it is the database that is being searched, not the Internet.

The different search engines are distinguished by how they catalog the data for your search.

• *AltaVista* (**www.altavista.com**) is one of the most popular search engines among business professionals (see Figure 3-22). When AltaVista first appeared it was revolutionary in its approach. Until then, only the title or concept of a web page might be cataloged, but not its contents. AltaVista strives to be a full-text index of every Internet page it accepts. It catalogs every word appearing on a web page. That means that if you are searching for a technical term that may not appear in the title of a page but appears in the text, AltaVista can find it and present it

**Figure 3-23.** Infoseek's reengineered search engine.

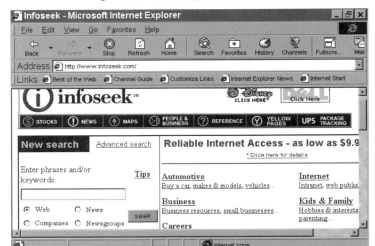

to you. Currently, Alta Vista claims to have 100 million Internet pages indexed.

• *Infoseek* (**www.infoseek.com**), another popular business engine, has recently been reengineered to search deeply into the actual text of web pages as well (see Figure 3-23).

• *Lycos* (**www.lycos.com**) indexes the title, headings, subheadings, and hyperlinks to other sites and the first twenty lines of text (see Figure 3-24).

• *HotBot* (**www.hotbot.com**) is the front-end search engine for probably the largest and fastest searchable index, called Inktomi. It allows you to confine your search to domain names, news sites, classified ads, stocks, newsgroups, and shareware (see Figure 3-25).

**Figure 3-24.** The Lycos search engine page is promoted as a reference guide for the Web.

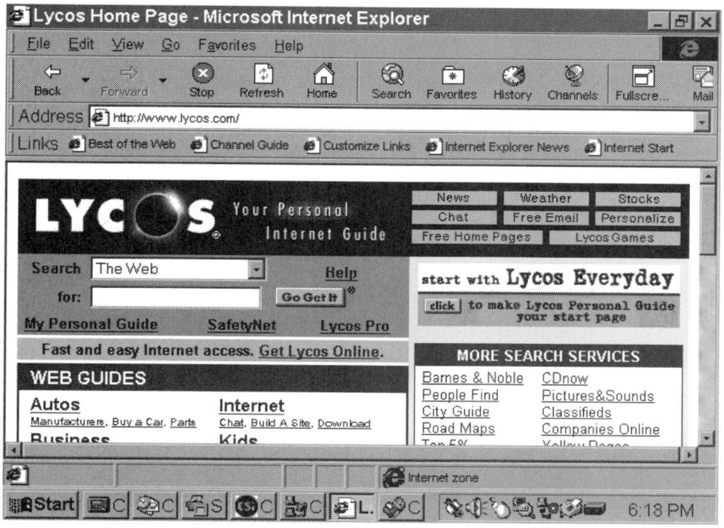

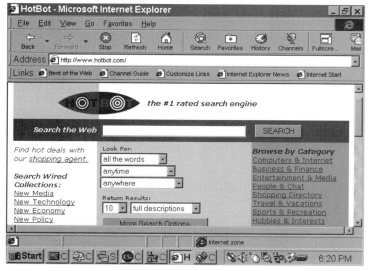

**Figure 3-25.** The HotBot search engine is unique in that it doesn't categorize web content like other search engines.

**Figure 3-26.** Excite uses concept-based searching and automatically finds synonyms for your search terms.

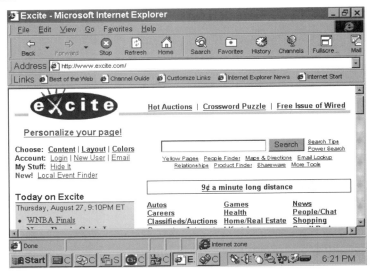

Excite screen display Copyright © 1995-1998 Excite, Inc. Reprinted with permission.

- *Excite* (**www.excite.com**) uses concept-based searching and will search on synonyms without your having to enter them. You will get results on the concept the search engine thinks you want, even though there might not be an exact match to the keywords you gave it (see Figure 3-26).

## Types of Search Engines

You will find several kinds of search engines available: simple, meta, and, for lack of an official term, super-duper.

- A **simple search engine** searches its own database. AltaVista is an example of a simple search engine.

- A **metasearch or parallel search engine** searches more than one database with your request. Inference Find (**www.infind.com**) will submit

**Figure 3-27.** Inference Find is a metasearch engine that lets you search across multiple search engines in one shot. You get less targeted but larger volume results.

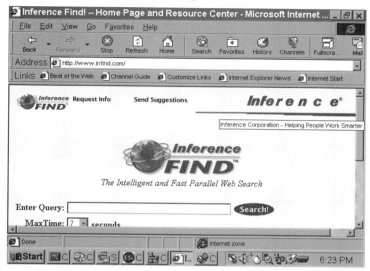

Reprinted with permission of Inference Corporation.

your request to the top six directories and search engines (Yahoo!, Excite, Lycos, WebCrawler, AltaVista, and Infoseek) and return to you a single list of results (see Figure 3-27).

You can hit six birds with one stone. That's the good news. The bad news is that metasearchers use the lowest common denominator in terms of search features. They have to use the features that are common to all the directories and engines to which they submit your request. It means you won't get as much tailoring in the search results, but you will get more volume and variety. No one engine can cover the entire Internet, so parallel searches can be of value.

- A **super-duper search engine** allows you to make your request in the form of a question. My current favorite is AskJeeves (**www.askjeeves.com**). Using natural language queries, it searches several databases as well as its

**Figure 3-28.** Ask Jeeves uses natural language queries but works best when you have simple, direct questions that return equally simple answers and facts.

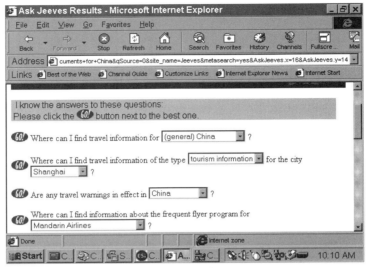

own, and it gives you back choices as to where to seek the answer (see Figure 3-28).

You must structure the request to make the best use of the tool. This is not the place for asking philosophical questions such as, "Why is there air?" or "What is the meaning of life?" Ask simple and direct questions (e.g., "What documents do I need for travel to China?"). If you ask the right questions, the results can be amazing. It actually makes you think there's a live person in there answering your questions for you. It may be so realistic you'll be tempted to start a conversation (e.g., "Hi there! You did such a great job with that last search. Thank you so much. This time my boss is going to China, and you know how those trips are to coordinate! I wish I worked for someone more organized. Anyway, I need to know . . ."). Of course, this is exaggeration, but starting your query with phrases such as "I need to know how to find . . ." or "I'm looking for . . ." are not necessary and make the search time longer. Cut to the chase. There really is no Jeeves at the AskJeeves site. Too bad. He seems like a nice guy!

### *Information to Know: Simple Search Engines*

| | |
|---|---|
| AltaVista (**www.altavista.com**) | Sophisticated, in-depth searching |
| Infoseek (**www.infoseek.com**) | Fastest in-depth searching |
| Excite (**www.excite.com**) | Works well with hard-to-define concept searches |
| EuroSeek (**www.euroseek.net**) | European search engine |
| Lycos (**www.lycos.com**) | Can limit your search to the top 5 percent websites as ranked by Lycos reviewers |
| HotBot (**www.hotbot.com**) | Largest search engine |
| The Argus Clearinghouse (**www.clearinghouse.net**) | Built by the University of Michigan's School of Information and Library Studies for serious research |
| Librarian's Index to the Internet (**sunsite.berkeley.edu/InternetIndex**) | In a word: amazing! |
| Shopfind (**www.shopfind.com**) | Searches for cyberstores, or sites on the Internet where you can buy stuff |

### *Information to Know: Metasearch Engines*

| | |
|---|---|
| Inference Find | **www.inferencefind.com/ifind** |
| MetaCrawler | **www.metacrawler.com** |
| MetaFind | **www.metafind.com** |
| Search.com | **www.search.com** |
| HuskySearch | **huskysearch. cs.washington.edu** |
| Mamma | **www.mamma.com** |
| Savvy Search | **savvysearch.com** |
| Dogpile | **www.dogpile.com** |

I'm not sure I want to know where they get these names, but as long as the tool works well for you, who cares what they call it!

### *Information to Know: Super-Duper Search Engines*

| | |
|---|---|
| AskJeeves | **www.askjeeves.com** |
| Findout | **www.findout.com** |

## Questions to Ask: Evaluating Search Engines

Most people have a favorite search engine. To evaluate new ones that come along, use these criteria:

- What kind of information is being indexed (e.g., concepts, titles, complete text)?

- How often is new information added (e.g., daily, weekly, hourly)?
- Is the information provided in the results header enough, and is it relevant and useful to me?
- Can I use sophisticated searches using Boolean functions (AND, OR, NOT), phrase searching, wild cards, and ranking, not just keyword searches?
- Do the help screens help?
- Is the search speed acceptable?
- Is it a directory or a search engine?

## I Just Need to Find Something! Where Do I Start?

With more and more sophisticated software available today, directories and search engines appear to be almost identical on your screen. They both have a fill-in-the-blank bar for you to type in keywords and search terms. Many other features look the same. It is getting harder and harder to tell them apart. Here's the difference.

## The Difference Between Directories and Search Engines and When to Use Each

A directory represents a hierarchical organization of information. The folks running the directory have made choices about how all this Internet stuff should be best organized to serve you. A directory gives you a path to follow from general area to specific location, from concept to concrete information. When you "search" in a directory, you are searching the organizational structure, looking for the right section of the store, so to speak. Remember you are searching on directory names here, not Internet page text as you would in a search engine. A general term might serve you better than a more specific one. If you call the department store and ask for the section of the store that sells a particular brand, they might not know where to send you. If you ask for women's clothing, they can help you.

In preparing to write this book, I did an informal survey. I found that about 50 percent of the experts say to start with a directory, it's easier.

The other 50 percent vote for starting with a search engine and tell you that is easier. There is no right or wrong answer, although people seem to be willing to fight to the death to defend their choice. This is just like buying a pair of shoes (will we ever stop shopping in this book?). You have to try them on and walk around in them to see how they fit.

As a general rule of thumb, if you are not sure of what you are looking for or are trying to see the big picture, a directory would be the best choice. If you are looking for a specific nugget of information, a search engine would serve you better.

## Newsgroups

Internet newsgroups (referred to collectively as USENET) are an important resource for you. They provide a forum for people interested in a particular topic to post messages (articles) about the topic. USENET stands for Users Network. Think of it as a huge online bulletin board where people's ideas, opinions, and expertise are available to you. These groups are not the place for pure research, but they are a source of information.

There are two types of newsgroups: moderated and unmoderated. A moderated group means that someone "owns" the group and weeds out unwanted content (i.e., advertising or articles not related to the topic). Unmoderated groups are not as focused.

The name "newsgroup" would lead you to think that they have something to do with newspapers, but this is not true, although the messages people post are called articles.

To access newsgroups, you will need newsreader software, but the good news is that both Microsoft Internet Explorer and Netscape Navigator provide this software as part of the browser.

Newsreader software not only gives you the ability to read the postings, but it also keeps track of which ones you have read so they are not presented to you the next time. The software should allow you to mark postings you want to read and then read those on-screen or offline.

If you want to find out what customers are saying about your product, look for a related-interest newsgroup, read the entries, and, if you wish, post a message. An offer of assistance would be an acceptable message, but an advertisement would not. (See Chapter 4 on Netiquette). Let's say your company manufactures yarn. You would look for crafts groups or knitting and needlework discussions. Many companies, Hewlett-Packard, for one, use newsgroups/discussion groups as one way to offer ongoing, cost-effective customer support. It also allows a company to readily see where customers are having problems and to fix them before they become more widespread.

Anyone can participate in a newsgroup just by connecting to the group using a browser. Before you connect, however, make sure that connection to newsgroups is not a violation of company policy, as some companies limit their access. The general heading types of newsgroups are:

| | |
|---|---|
| *alt* | alternative |
| *biz* | business |
| *comp* | computers |
| *misc* | miscellaneous |
| *news* | news |
| *rec* | recreational-related topics |
| *sci* | science-related topics |
| *soc* | social topics |
| *talk* | discussions |

These heading types are called hierarchies and are the first part of the newsgroup's name. Then you have topic and subtopic, with name parts separated by a dot (.)—for example, biz.finance.stocks.

**Figure 3-29.** Deja News is a popular USENET search engine and directory.

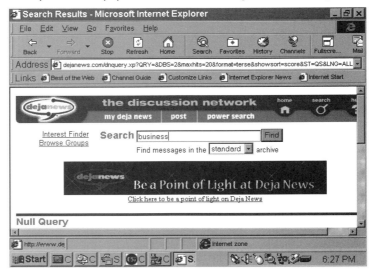

Reprinted with permission of Deja News.

## Finding the Newsgroup You Want

Directories such as Deja News (**www.dejanews.com**), Cyber Fiber News-groups (**www.cyberfiber.com**), or the Liszt of Newsgroups (**www.listz. com/news**) are good sources for finding newsgroups and messages in which you might have an interest. Figure 3-29 shows the Deja News site.

These newsgroup directories use a searching system that allows you to search on a word or phrase. You can search for current messages, usually no more than two months old, or for archived messages (posts) that contain your keywords.

## Your First Newsgroup Message

Once you do post that first message to a newsgroup, you will probably get a response. If you want to reply, don't start a new e-mail message.

**Figure 3-30.** Deja News allows you to limit or filter your search according to different criteria such as date or subject.

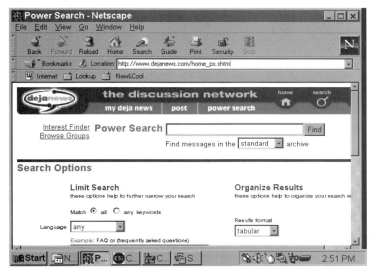

That would break the "thread" that links the original message and the responses to it.

Without the thread, it is difficult for readers to follow the sequence of messages. If several people respond, it is impossible to keep track. With the message on your screen, use the reply function provided you. You can compose an answer that will connect to the thread of the topic.

## Filtering

In searching for a newsgroup you can also save yourself a great deal of time by filtering your request (see Figure 3-30). To filter a search is to narrow it down, using specific criteria such as date or subject.

## Flaming

People in newsgroups can be very passionate about the particular opinions and ideas they support. If someone responds in anger to a posted message, this is called flaming. Just as the name implies, it's not something you want to do or perpetuate. You are too professional for that anyway.

## Discussion Groups

Discussion groups, also called discussion lists or mailing lists, are e-mail-based discussions of different topics. The difference between a newsgroup and a discussion group is that in a newsgroup, the messages reside on the host machine and you go to the newsgroup server to look at them. If you subscribe to a discussion group/list, you are sent a copy of every e-mail message posted to the list. That can result in a flood of e-mail that you may not need or want to see.

If you wish to join a discussion group/list, subscribing is as easy as filling out an on-screen form or sending a message to the administrative address given with the word "Subscribe" typed in the body or subject line of the message. The instructions will tell you exactly what to do to subscribe and, in some cases, how to unsubscribe (see Figure 3-31).

If you are offered the option to receive your messages in "digest" form, take it. That means the messages will not be sent individually, but condensed together into digest pages and sent weekly. It makes for much less e-mail and yet allows easy access to the information.

To search for a list of discussion groups, go to the Publicly Accessible Mailing Lists website (see Figure 3-32) at **www.neosoft.com/internet/paml**. Once you get to the list, click on the subject you want and you'll see the available groups/lists.

You can also look for mailing lists through your favorite search engine. A third alternative is to send an e-mail to listserv@listserv.net. Do not include a subject or signature line. In the message box, simply type the words "list global/" followed by whatever subject you want a list on (e.g., list global/travel). You will then receive by e-mail a list of discussion groups on the subject you are interested in.

After you sign up for a particular list, the first e-mail you receive will be a confirmation of your joining the list and the instructions for how to cancel your subscription if you wish. Keep that message for later refer-

**Figure 3-31.** Discussion groups give specific instructions for how to subscribe to them via e-mail. **TIP:** LISTSERV and Majordomo are two terms you'll see often, referring to the two programs for managing mailing list servers.

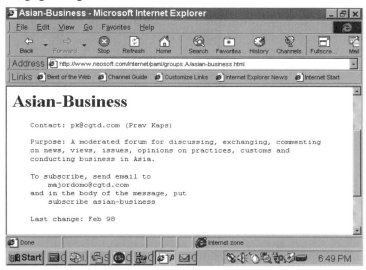

**Figure 3-32.** A great shopping site for discussion groups is the Publicly Accessible Mailing Lists website, where you can browse by category or use a search form.

ence. Just as in newsgroups, you will find both moderated and unmoderated lists. Choosing a moderated list is to your advantage because the content will be more focused and will stay on target.

## Announcement-Only Mailing Lists

If you want to receive vendor information automatically, you might find announcement-only mailing lists useful. These are usually presented to you as part of a web page with an offer to send you information, updates, or other tips via e-mail. Ziff-Davis, a publisher in the computer industry, offers mailing lists (see Figure 3-33) that send weekly usage tips on products such as Windows CE 2.0 and Microsoft Office 97.

## Internet Relay Chat

Internet Relay Chat (IRC) is the protocol that allows you to connect to a chat server and type messages to others in real time. Internet phone and video chat services also make use of IRC. A site that helps you find chat rooms is Talk City (**www.talkcity.com**). You can also use your search engine and search for "chat AND" the topic you want to chat about.

The difference between a chat room and a newsgroup/discussion group is that chatting occurs in real time and the conversation scrolls on and off the screen as it is taking place. Newsgroups/discussion groups don't send messages in real time; they work more like the office bulletin board: You leave me a message, then I leave you a response, and both messages stay on the board until cleanup time.

For the moment, chat rooms appear to have little business application outside your company intranet (see Chapter 6), although there are a growing number of chat channels on recreational topics. AOL's top chat event for 1998 was a conversation with Koko, a 310-pound gorilla who spoke sign language to a human translator who worked the chat room.

## Gopher

Gopher is a subset of the Internet reported to be the first usable directory system. It works with a system of menus using its own protocol to note and locate material stored on Gopher servers.

**Figure 3-33.** Ziff-Davis (ZD) offers announcement-only e-mail services with tips on using many kinds of popular software.

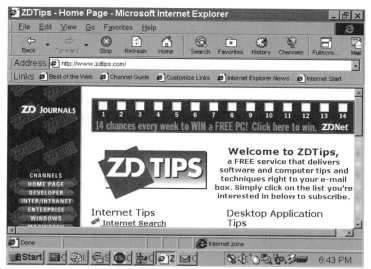

Rumor has it that the reason it is called Gopher is that the first Gopher site was developed at the University of Minnesota, where the mascot is the Golden Gopher. You need to remember that Gopher sites are technically not real web pages—they are menus. Therefore, they look and work differently.

The majority of Gopher sites are hosted by government and educational servers and are called Gopher holes. If you are given a Gopher address, type it into the Location or Address bar of your browser, and the browser will take you there. The Library of Congress (**www.loc.gov**), for example, uses a Gopher server to provide information on hours of operation and reader registration (**gopher://marvel.loc.gov**). You will see that in the address **http://** has been replaced by **gopher://**. Because this system doesn't use the Hypertext Transfer Protocol, it technically is part of the Internet but not the Web, where only HTTP is spoken.

**Figure 3-34.** To do a keyword search of a Gopher directory, a Jughead search may be an option.

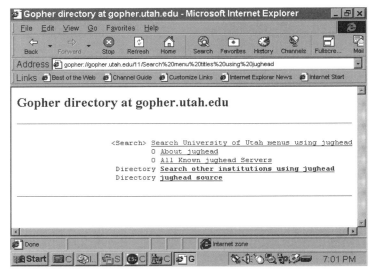

Reprinted with permission of the University of Utah.

Many libraries use Gopher directories to allow you access to research materials. If you see an icon—a symbol that looks like a pair of binoculars—next to a directory listing, it means that you can use a keyword search in that part of the Gopher directory. Files can be used on-screen or downloaded for later use.

You may have heard the comic-book names Veronica, Jughead, and Archie associated with Gopher files.

Veronica is a set of software tools developed to help you search through Gopher menus. It stands for (believe it or not) Very Easy Rodent-Oriented Netwide Index to Computerized Archives.

Jughead is the name of a program that facilitates keyword searches in Gopher (see Figure 3-34).

Archie is a network system that helps you locate files stored on FTP (File Transfer Protocol) servers. FTP, like Gopher and HTTP, is another

Internet protocol often used for sending and receiving large files. You might be given an address of a server site from which you need to download a software upgrade (ftp:microsoft.com/softlib). Instead of the address starting with **http://**, it will start with **ftp:**. All it means is that you will be using that protocol to dial into an FTP server that houses the software you want.

Unless you are doing highly specialized research, what you want is probably available to you through your favorite web search engine. You won't need to go to these systems, so you can put those Sunday funnies away. As long as you are using either Microsoft Internet Explorer or Netscape Navigator as your browser, they will be able to communicate using all these protocols—HTTP, FTP, and Gopher—and others. The good news is that you won't have to do anything special. The browser will do it all.

# Chapter 4

# Netiquette

Some travelers, when they get to the airport, transform themselves from being gracious and polite people to I don't know what, but I don't want to be in an airport with it. They instantly forget every manner their mother taught them, and their behavior deteriorates completely. Apparently the anonymity of the Net has the same effect for some people and seems to encourage them to behave in a less than professional manner.

This chapter describes Netiquette: what it is and some good rules of thumb to follow. There are suggestions for polite behavior using e-mail, discussion groups, newsgroups, and chat sessions. You'll also find some security practices just in case you need them.

Netiquette combines the words *network* and *etiquette* to describe a set of behavior rules for being on the Internet. Our manners and behavior define us to others. This is most important on the Internet because people don't see us; they interact with us electronically. Others make their impressions of us by seeing the documents and messages we send. If the grammar and spelling are incorrect, that sends a message. If your communication is rambling and unfocused, then that relays a lack of respect for the reader. One

**Figure 4-1.** The home page of the Internet Computer Security Association offers a downloadable guide for managing your employees Internet access and use.

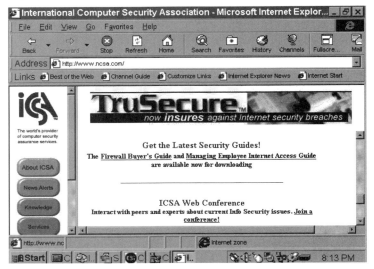

Reprinted with permission of the Internet Computer Security Association.

of the best tests you can use is to ask yourself, "Would Mom approve?" If you can pass the "mom" test, you are usually home free.

## Acceptable Use

The first place to look before you get online is to your company's acceptable use policy (AUP) for technology. This contains guidelines for using your organization's technology in a professional manner. Your mom had guidelines: "Sit up straight," "Clean your plate," "Don't jump off a bridge just because all your friends are doing it." You remember. Well, any company that allows Internet access has guidelines to direct its use. They should include appropriate use of e-mail; Internet fax; messaging to newsgroups, discussion groups, and chat areas; security procedures; and rules for transmitting, storing, and retrieving information.

If your company has no policy, you may want to put one together. Start with the same code of conduct and ethics you have in the rest of your workplace, and work from there. Make sure you keep in mind how the system should be used and its benefits. One company actually prohibited the electronic exchange of files. Since that's basically what you do on the Internet, why bother to turn your computer connection on?

You can get help establishing an Internet use policy from The Internet Computer Security Association (**www.icsa.com**). It can provide you a workbook on setting up policies and a guide for Internet access (see Figure 4-1).

If you use a service provider, it will have its own set of acceptable use policies that will be available to you online.

## Play Nice and Share Your Toys: E-Mail and Messaging Manners

If you are just using your web browser to access information, there really is no netiquette to worry about, because for the most part you are not interacting with anyone. When you are interacting with others using e-mail and messaging, then you have more to be concerned about. Mom used to say, "Actions speak louder than words." Unfortunately, Mom was wrong when it comes to the Net. Words speak the loudest. (I'm not going to be the one to tell her she was wrong!) The meaning of the message is in the mind of the reader, not yours. If you are having a face-to-face conversation with someone, more than 50 percent of the message is conveyed by body language and facial expression. With electronic messaging, however, the reader doesn't have those cues. They can't see that you're smiling and you didn't really mean it the way it sounded. So the reader makes an interpretation based primarily on content and personal feelings about the subject.

In the business world, unsolicited feedback and sarcasm can come across as criticism or, worse, disrespect. Those are two things to avoid in electronic communication, and business communication in general for that matter. Here's the acid test. Would you say the same thing if you were speaking with someone face to face? Would you want the world, your boss, your mom, to see this message? If you are in doubt, write a draft of your message and save it for later review before you send it. If it is a complicated issue, you might want someone else to review it as well. You are judged by the impression your words make, so make it a good one.

## E-Mail

**1.** Use the standard salutation you would use in any written business communication. Business is business, and you'll want to use the same formality you would with any communication sent on company stationery.

**2.** Always fill in the subject box on an e-mail message. It lets people know the importance and the focus of your message.

**3.** Create an e-mail letterhead for messages you send outside your company. This clues the reader that the communication is "official" and not a personal note from you. Letterhead can also be used to identify a specific team or initiative.

**4.** Only mark those messages urgent that are truly urgent. Some people will mark every message they send as urgent, which means that readers can't discriminate which do and which don't require immediate attention.

**5.** When generating messages, set your spell checker to automatically check the message before it is sent. If your system is able, let it check grammar as well. Don't make it an option you have to remember each time you compose a message.

**6.** Use the proper punctuation. You shouldn't need forty-seven exclamation points for impact. Let the richness of your verbiage do that.

**7.** Don't comment on a sender's spelling, punctuation, or grammar unless you are moonlighting as their high school English teacher.

**8.** If you are sending a URL in the body of your message, put it on a separate line. The newest systems will recognize a URL and create the link; however, older e-mail systems won't, and your recipient will find it much easier to cut and paste the link and transfer it to their browser if it is on a separate line.

**9.** If you think the recipient of your message uses an older e-mail system to retrieve messages or a small screen (e.g., a handheld or palm-size computer), limit the column width in which you type in your message.

**10.** If you add a "signature" to your messages, make it no more than four lines. Name, title, company, and e-mail address are traditional. Because abbreviations, or aliases, are sometimes used as e-mail IDs, signature blocks can be helpful to the reader.

**11.** Do not compose messages with the CAPS LOCK key on. This is interpreted as screaming at the reader.

**12.** Add a response line to your messages to let the reader know if you require a response in a certain time frame or if no response is necessary (NRN).

**13.** Let the reader know in the body of your message if you've included an attachment. If it doesn't arrive, the recipient will know something is missing.

**14.** Try not to create unnecessary traffic. Keep your messages focused and as short as is practical. You know how many messages you get on any given day; someone else might get even more. Some service providers based overseas charge their members per kilobyte of information. Some respect for their time and budget is in order.

**15.** Leave two lines of space between paragraphs. It makes the message easier to read and also makes it easier to respond using parts of the original message text if it is spaced.

**16.** Respond to e-mail promptly, even if it is just to say you'll give a full response later.

**17.** Respond like for like. If someone calls you and you e-mail a response, it might appear as if you didn't want to talk to the person. Unless you need to reply with a complicated document as an e-mail attachment, return a phone call message with a phone call.

**18.** Don't demand prompt responses from others. The value of e-mail is convenience, not immediacy.

**19.** Don't forward someone's message without the permission of the original sender. Don't send unsolicited e-mail or advertising. Chain letters are inappropriate.

**20.** Do make use of abbreviations to shorten a message. Commonly accepted abbreviations are:

| | |
|---|---|
| AFAIK | As far as I know |
| BTW | By the way |
| BYKT | But you knew that |
| FYI | For your information |
| HTH | Hope this helps |
| IAE | In any event |
| IMO | In my opinion |
| IMHO | In my humble opinion |
| IOW | In other words |
| IYSWIM | If you see what I mean |
| L8R | Later |
| LOL | Laughing out loud |
| NRN | No reply necessary |
| OBO | Or best offer |
| SYL | See you later |

TNSTAAFL  There's no such thing as a free lunch

TTYL      Talk to you later

TYVM      Thank you very much

WRT       With respect to

These abbreviations are typed in upper case letters so the recipient knows this is an abbreviation and not that your spell checker was turned off.

Don't use "smileys"—punctuation drawings that express emotion—in business correspondence.

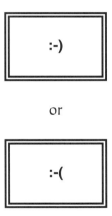

or

## Discussion Groups, Newsgroups, and Chat Rooms
• The first thing to do when you enter a newsgroup is to read through the messages so that you can get a sense of the topic material and acceptable communication behavior in this group. If there is a help or frequently asked questions (FAQ) section, read through that set of messages first. Usually if the question has already been answered, you don't want to ask it again. It would create unnecessary postings. If you have trouble finding the FAQ section, go to this site, **ftp://rtfm.mit.edu/pub/usenet-by-group**. It is run by the Massachusetts Institute of Technology and lists all the USENET

newsgroups by name. Scroll till you find the name of the group for whose FAQs you are looking and click.

• If you post a message and get back the response RTFAQ, you are being told to read the frequently asked questions.

• Avoid slang and acronyms. There may be international participants who would not have a language reference point for your comments.

• When you post messages, make sure you title them accurately and stay with the topic. Messages that deviate from the topic of the group are unwelcome.

• Newsgroups and discussion groups are not places to post jokes, personal messages, or advertisements.

• When you post a message, post it only once. More is not better in this case. In chat rooms, where you are posting messages in real time, it is courteous to let others finish their comments before you post yours, so don't interrupt.

• It's not appropriate to post someone else's private message in public space such as a discussion group.

• Your purpose may be to see what customers think of your product, so you may choose to read messages, but not contribute. Don't get emotionally involved trying to defend your cause or product. Be a good listener (i.e., reader), then post a solution or offer to help.

• Most groups have an "owner" who will post a message about rules or guidelines for the group. Make sure you review and abide by these rules.

• Never respond in anger. It's called flaming. You might think that because it is written, it would have a less negative response than a verbal attack. Actually, the opposite is true.

## Spam: It Isn't Just for Sandwiches Anymore

Spamming is defined as sending multiple unsolicited messages. Many times it is in the form of advertising, or publicity, like junk e-mail. It can show up in discussion groups, newsgroups, and chat rooms as well. To force-feed unwanted information on the Net is considered very bad form, much worse than elbows on the table according to Mom. In fact, some vendors and service sites on the Internet use the fact that they fight spam as part of their publicity to get you to join their forums. Do not use newsgroups, discussion groups, or chat rooms to sell a product. It's not what the participants are there to discuss.

If you are the victim of spamming, there is a website that can help. The Internet E-Mail Marketing Council (**www.iemmc.org**) is a group made up of large bulk e-mail companies. They will take requests at their website to have your address removed from their lists. However, if you are being spammed by a nonmember, this organization can't help you.

## Security

When browsing on the Internet, the main issue is to be sure you follow your company's rules regarding which sites you access and for what purpose. Security is an issue of prime concern to your system administrator, and you already follow all the security policies to the letter.

What if you are in a small office and have no system administrator, let alone security policies? Get some, quick!

### Information to Know: About Security

• *Backup.* Have a regular backup schedule and keep to it. Allow intervals to extend only to the amount of work that could be re-created painlessly if necessary. Trust me, you will see the value of having a regular backup schedule if you ever have to re-create more than a few hours' worth of work. It's not a question of if you will need your backup copy, but when. This does not mean "when I get around to it" or the "first Thursday of every month beginning with Z." It means twice a day, every day, no fooling. Use a set of disks or tapes in rotation. That way if your latest backup copy is corrupt (i.e., dysfunctional, not dishonest), then the backup before that one may be okay and you won't have lost too much work.

- ***Antivirus software.*** Make sure you have it, use it, and update it frequently. Don't disable the virus scan to make your boot-up process go faster. That's like . . . well, never mind what it's like, just don't do it!

- ***Secure browsers.*** Make sure your browser complies with Internet security standards. The most recent versions of Netscape Navigator and Microsoft Internet Explorer (versions 3.0 and greater) support secure connections. You can tell whether your browser is secure if it displays a pop-up message whenever you are about to enter a secure area. Internet Explorer also displays the image of a lock on the status bar at the bottom of the browser screen when you enter a secure area. Similarly, Netscape Navigator displays the image of a broken key when you are not in a secure area and a whole key when you are in a secure area.

- ***Online shoppers beware.*** If you are going to buy a product over the Internet, make sure you are shopping at the website of a reputable company. If you have doubts, ask your local consumer protection agency or search the Better Business Bureau online (**www.bbb.com**). Also, if you feel uncomfortable giving your credit card number over the Internet, don't. Legitimate electronic vendors will offer secure servers or the option to call your order in on a toll-free number.

- ***Just say no.*** When you are on the Internet and you are asked for information that you think is unnecessary or should not be made public, just say, "No thank you." Would you print your Social Security number on a billboard alongside the highway?

- ***Keep a secret.*** There are relatively inexpensive software packages that can encrypt the data you have stored on your system and require a password for access. This security measure protects your data not only while the machine is in the office, but also if it is stolen.

- ***Password protection.*** Don't give your password to anyone or publicize anyone else's password. The best passwords are meaningless nonsense. Don't choose passwords that are related to your personal life, such as your birthday or your dog's name, for example, that someone else may be able to easily guess.

• **_Privacy._** Remember that no information on the Net is private. I don't care how many guarantees and promises you have. Once you put information out there, the potential exists that the world can see it, whether that's your intention or not. You are much safer to work under the assumption that everyone can see your communication. Make Mom proud and only share information and communications online that you wouldn't be embarrassed to have her read.

# Chapter 5

# Effective Searching: Delegating Tasks to Your New Assistant

Imagine your office filing system. On second thought, don't—that's too scary. Picture an imaginary office filing system where everyone files his or her own materials with no structure, rhyme, or reason. Every folder is just stuffed into a file drawer at random, and two new cabinets are arriving and are filled every day. Documents are frequently moved or destroyed, but no one is notified because no one is in charge. (Take a deep breath and remember that this is not your office!)

Yet this is an apt description of how information is stored on the Internet. How do you find anything in that mess? You don't. Delegate the job of searching to your online assistant.

This chapter looks at the logic of a good Internet search and offers you both tools and examples.

As you saw in Chapter 3, you have access to some wonderful tools to help you with the awesome task of finding your needle in a haystack. But the most important tool is you, and the thought process you apply to your searching effort before you go online. The more tailored and specific a search is, the more usable the information is that you receive.

Think of this as delegation. You are delegating this "legwork" to your assistant, the Internet. Just as you wouldn't delegate work to a human assistant without first applying some thought, planning, and communication, the same applies to the Internet. The steps of good delegation are to:

1. Think through the task.

2. Write up the task.

3. Look for the right delegatee (in this case, internet tool) for the job.

4. Communicate the task and provide the tools necessary to accomplish it.

5. Monitor and correct along the way.

6. Learn from this process for the next time.

## Think Through the Task

The first thing you do is to define the target. Ask who, what, where, how, when, and why questions to define your topic. Establish what information you need to find and how it will be used. Make sure you have a clear understanding of what usable information would look like before you go searching for it. Would success mean lots of information, a specific set of facts or figures, a previously undiscovered resource? If this is someone else's request, it may also help you to know what they intend to do with the information so you can structure your online search and search results accordingly.

## Write Up the Task

Take the time to put your thought process on paper. One way to write up the task is to create a searching grid (see Figure 5-1) that you can use to formulate your search keywords and the results you seek.

**Figure 5-1.** The successful searching grid is a worksheet to help you formulate your search strategy on paper before you go online. Here is an example of a search strategy for finding a chemical manufacturer.

| |
|---|
| **Define the target:**<br>Chemical supplier in Chicago area that provides alkylation process<br>**Define the success:**<br>Get the company name, phone number, e-mail address |
| **How will this information be used?**<br>Give to purchasing department to add to our supplier list |
| **Keywords:**<br>　**Include:**<br>Chicago, company, chemical, alkylation<br><br>　**Exclude:** |
| **Word strings or phrases:**<br>"chemical company" "alkylation process" |
| **Query/request structure**<br>chemical + company +"alkylation process"<br>Chicago + chemical + alkylation |
| **Preferred Tools:** AltaVista, Hoovers Online, Dun & Bradstreet, Dialog |

## Inclusions

Assemble a list or mind map of keywords. Look for the keywords you would use to distinguish your target. How was it described to you? How would you describe it to someone else? Are there any terms you want to include that make this target unique, make it stand out?

**Example:** Your boss is trying to find a company that she has heard about. She doesn't know the name, but knows the firm is in the Chicago area, is a chemical manufacturer, and offers a process called alkylation. Keywords would be *company, Chicago, chemical, alkylation*. If you need to broaden your list, use your dictionary and thesaurus for synonyms. Include variations of the keywords such as plurals, and use wildcard Boolean search characters that help you find alternate spellings of your keywords. (See the section on "Boolean Operators" later in this chapter.)

## Exclusions

Also look for exclusions. Are there any words you should exclude to help narrow the search?

**Example:** Your boss is traveling to Turkey and wants some background information before his trip. If you used only the keyword "Turkey" for your search, AltaVista will return 780,360 matches. Unlike a particular spouse who shall remain nameless, the Internet listens carefully to every keyword you give it. The results returned include not only information about the country of Turkey but also restaurants with "turkey" in their name, the Turkey Scramble cycling event, and turkey trivia. There are thousands of recipes for using leftover turkey including "Turkey Revenge Soup" (I was afraid to look) and references to brand-name liquor with "turkey" in the title. Some of the references are actually in Turkish, so I don't know exactly what they are. Just by adding one exclusion ("not recipes"), the search results are cut by more than half. In the simple search box, type in:

```
Turkey −recipes
```

Please notice that there is a space between the first word *Turkey* and the minus (-) sign, but not between the minus (-) sign and the word *recipes*.

## Strings or Phrases

Develop word strings or phrases. Think of descriptive two- or three-word phrases that might be in the text of the web page.

**Example:** What does the boss want to know about traveling to Turkey? Travel warnings? Doing business in Turkey? Travel documents required? A search for "travel documents" and Turkey yielded 51,330 matches, with the best site ranked number one. Put the word string within quotation marks so that it is the phrase and not each individual word you search.

**Figure 5-2.** WebCrawler is one of many search directories on the Internet you can use when you are starting with a broad concept and need help narrowing it down.

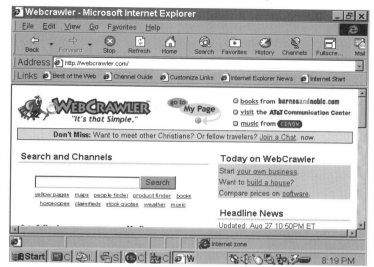

Copyright © 1995-1998. Reprinted with permission of Excite, Inc.

## Look for the Right Tool for the Job

Just as you would look for the right person for the task, you'll want to choose the right tool for your search.

• ***If you have the specific web address that you want to go to, your browser is your first choice.*** Just type the address into the location or address box and go. If you have a company name but not its web address, a good bet is to try **http://www.companyname.com.** The actual company name should be written in all lower case letters and run together, no spaces (e.g., **www.kraftfoods.com**). Chances are very good that you'll land on their home page first shot.

• ***If you have a concept but do not have precise terms to describe it, use a directory.*** Yahoo!, Net Guide, and WebCrawler (see Figure 5-2) are popular directories you can start with. The task here would be exploring a topic in general and allowing the directory to help you see the big picture or narrow it down. (See Chapter 3 for information on using directories.)

 • *If you are looking for a person or company address, also try a directory*. Certain search directories such as Bigfoot (**www.bigfoot.com**) are designed to help you track down e-mail and street addresses. Other directories provide only reviews, annotations, or descriptions of a wide variety of other sites. However, looking through these abstracts may help you to evaluate whether a website might have what you are looking for.

 • *If you have keywords and want a specific piece of information, go straight to your favorite simple search engine.* AltaVista, HotBot, Excite, and others listed in Chapter 3 are simple search engines.
 A word of caution, though: Just as in the office, everyone delegates to the person who performs ("Give it to Mikey, he'll do it!"). If you always go straight to your same trusty search engine first, you may be missing out on a shorter search or better results somewhere else.

 • *If you get too few results or off-target results, go to one of the metasearch engines.* Metasearch websites let you perform a search across multiple search engines in parallel. Inference Find (**www.infind.com**) is a metasearch engine.

 • *If you can form a simple question, use natural language searchers.* A simple question is something such as "What travel documents do I need to go to Turkey?" that has a simple or factual answer.

 • *If you would normally go to a paper source, check if your favorite reference book has an online equivalent.* Would you normally go out and buy a Frommer's travel guide, or pull your *Hoover's Handbook* off the bookshelf? Both have online versions of their information (**www.frommers.com** and **www.hoovers.com**, respectively), and chances are that other of your favorite paper references are also available on the Internet. The value of that text being online is not that you can read it page by page on the screen, but that it is searchable.

## Specialized Databases

There is another set of resources on the Net to be aware of, and these are called subscriber or specialized databases. As the name implies, you (or hopefully your company) pay a subscription fee to be able to search these databases. Dialog, InSite Pro, and LEXIS-NEXIS are three of the best known. These databases are tailored to business professionals. They have their own searching techniques, so they are somewhat more complicated and obtuse than the basic search engines we have mentioned. If you work in a larger company, your corporate librarian can usually do this kind of searching for you if you are unable to find what you need on your own.

An example might be when you need to compile background information and financial reports on a company that your boss is thinking of acquiring. You would need to obtain not only annual reports, but proxy statements, disclosure reports, and documents filed with the Securities and Exchange Commission. Although using a dedicated single source is costly, it allows you to reduce the time and effort spent trying to retrieve that information.

### *Information to Know: Specialty Databases*

| | |
|---|---|
| Brainwave for NewsNet (**www.newsnet.telebase.com/brainwave**) | Corporate profiles, industry newsletters, access to credit reporting |
| Knowx (**www.knowx.com**) | Draws its information from public records (i.e., legal judgments, real estate documents, DBA [doing business as] filings) |
| Paper Chase (**www.paperchase.com**) | Health care and medical information |
| WESTLAW (**www.westpub.com**) | Legal resources |
| Dialog (**www.dialog.krinfo.com**) | Specialty information for scientists, engineers, patent attorneys, and other business professionals |

**Figure 5-3.** Northern Light lets you simultaneously search both the Web at large and a collection of specialty databases. Some information is free. Other information requires either a per-article or a membership fee for access.

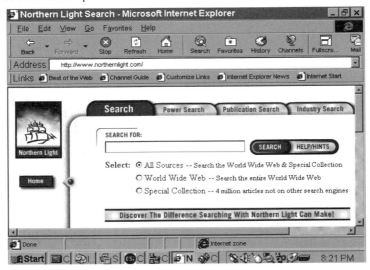

Reprinted with permission of Northernlight Technology.

InSite Pro (**www.informationaccess.com**)    Categorized by business, market, computer, consumer, and newsletter databases

LEXIS-NEXIS (**www.lexis-nexis.com**)    Legal information sources as well as news and business sources

Some databases will allow you a first-level search free of charge to show you what you could see if you were willing to subscribe. Northern Light (**www.nlsearch.com**) offers a free search engine, free abstracts, and access to what they call their special collection (see Figure 5-3).

This collection is made up of articles that Northern Light states are not available elsewhere on the Internet. They charge either a per-article or a membership fee for access to the collection. The results of a search are presented to you in custom folders that categorize results based on your search request.

## Communicate the Task and Provide the Necessary Tools for Accomplishing It

For the most part, a single word search of a directory will give you workable results, but a similar search using a search engine would probably yield too many results and you would be overwhelmed. A search engine can actually filter some of the results, but you first need to tell it what you want.

During the step of writing up your task and formulating your thought process, you assembled keywords, exclusions, and phrases. With these in hand, head for the help menu or a box marked search tips. All search engines should have tips for doing a simple or advanced search. This is where you will find the syntax that this particular search engine uses. Syntax is crucial here. For example, if you search on the words *team building*, the results returned will show links to the word *team* and links to the word *building*. However, if the phrase *"team building"* is entered as a search string encased in quotes, it will cause the search tool to limit the list of results to web pages in which the word *team* and the word *building* are found side by side. You might wish to look for vendors online that sell office supplies at a discount. The syntax would be:

---

**"office supplies" +discount**

---

**Note that the syntax requires a space before the plus sign ( + ) but not between the + and the word that follows it. You are tailoring the search to look for web pages that have the phrase *office supplies* and also contain the word *discount*.**

**Figure 5-4.** The AltaVista advanced search screen has a fill-in box for writing special Boolean searches. You can also limit your search to specific date ranges.

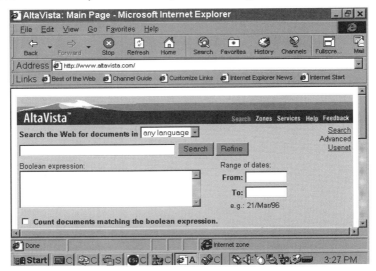

Reprinted with permision of Compaq Corporation.

## Advanced Searching

You should also explore the advanced search capabilities of your favorite engine. For each product this area is titled differently and may be called an advanced search or a super search, for example. Some superlative will indicate to you that this is more than just your simple search area. In the advanced search area, you will see a fill-in-the-blank box. You also may see a block marked Boolean (see Figure 5-4). This is a space where you can fill in what are called Boolean operators.

### Boolean Operators

If you remember high school algebra (a memory that I, for one, have personally blocked out completely), you'll remember the term *Boolean*.

Named for mathematician George Boolean, Boolean search terms (or Booleans, for short) are terms you can use to tailor a search (see Figure 5-5–5-7).

**AND**     Example: cats and dogs. Returns pages in which both the words *cat* and *dog* occur.

**Figure 5-5.** The results of a Boolean AND search.

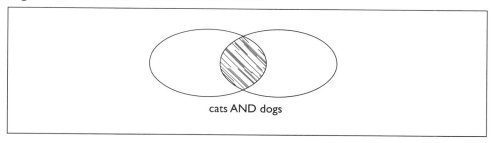

**OR**     Example: car or automobile. Returns results in which one or the other word occurs, so that includes all *car* references and all *automobile* references. This type of search is useful if you don't know which term may be used.

**Figure 5-6.** The results of a Boolean OR search.

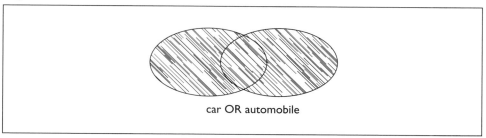

**NOT**     Example: turkey not recipes. Not searches are used for exclusion. This is the same request as the **Turkey −recipes** syntax we used previ-

**(In an AltaVista advanced search, the syntax is "and not.")**

ously in the simple search, but now we are using the Boolean operator. It will return results in which the word *turkey* but not the word *recipe* are used.

**Figure 5-7.** The results of a Boolean NOT search.

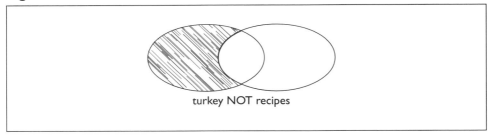

turkey NOT recipes

**NEAR**      Example: clipart near business. This is also referred to as a proximity search, and it returns results in which the word *clipart* appears within ten words of *business* in either direction.

## Other Tailoring Tools

**Nesting**      Example: (ticket or fare) and "lowest price." Keywords are nested together with parentheses to establish the order of search and the combination or exclusion of different topics (it's looking more like algebra every minute!). The words *ticket* and *fare* are each searched for separately, then each individually combined with

**Figure 5-8.** Nesting is a search technique that allows different inclusions or exclusions of keywords and phrases. It yields different results depending on whether you are combining a NOT search with an OR search, or a NOT search with an AND search.

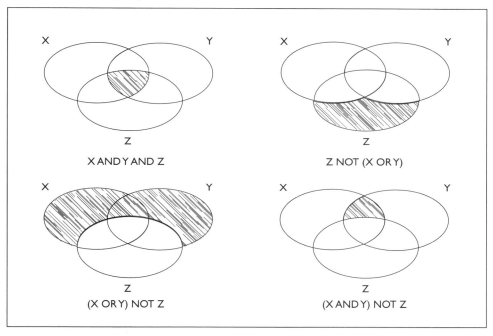

the phrase *"lowest price."* So you actually searched for *ticket* and *"lowest price"* as well as *fare* and *"lowest price"* (see Figure 5-8).

**Wildcards** Example: (ticket* or fare) and "lowest price." Wildcard searches yield variations of a root word. The asterisk (*) at the end of the word *ticket* returns the words *tickets, ticketing,* and *ticketed.* You get the picture.

**Date** Many search engines also allow you to limit your search results by date range (e.g., from August 14, 1998 to January 1, 1999).

For me to give additional searching specifics won't really help you, because although there are some similarities across all the search engines, every search site has its own set of rules and syntax. As an example, most searches are case insensitive. However, if you are in Infoseek and put in a proper name with its capitalization—George Washington—Infoseek will recognize it as such and search for it as a name, the two words together in that order with the capitalization. That is, in fact, an awesome feat for a search engine, since most searches tend to be very literal.

Rather than repeat myself, let me say this with emphasis. Retrieve the search instructions, tips, and help files for each search engine you use frequently. Save them in an electronic folder for referral.

## Monitor and Correct Along the Way

Once you have made your request, let's see what results you get back (see Figure 5-9). The list of items that meet your search criteria will include the following information:

| | |
|---|---|
| *Document title:* | Name of the web page |
| *Summary:* | Either a description of the page or the first few lines |
| *Ranking or score:* | A numerical value calculating relevancy to your request |
| *Hyperlink:* | Giving you "click on" access to the site |

Just as with people, you don't expect perfection the first time around. Don't be discouraged. Just remember that this is a process. In fact, your first search may give you excellent clues to develop better exclusions and phrases. If the first set of results from your search pop onto your screen and you hear yourself say, "Rats, I didn't want that," you can use the search results you got as the basis for more tailoring.

It is very likely that you will be presented with a large number of items that match your search criteria. Luckily for you, the results list that is

**Figure 5-9.** Search results returned by doing an AltaVista search for "American Management Association." The results include the source URL, a description, a hyperlink to the source, and date information.

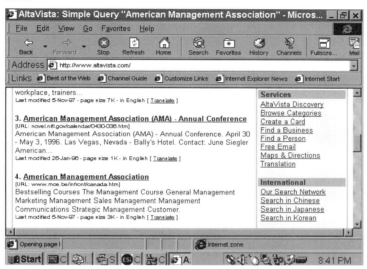

returned to you will be ranked by the placement and the occurrence rate of the search word(s) you input. The more frequently your search criteria appear in a site, the closer that site will be to the top of your results list. The tool is trying to determine which sites would be of most value. It will also give higher ranking to those in which your search words appear at the beginning of an article. You shouldn't have to look too far down the list to find what you are looking for, or to know you are totally off base and need to start again.

While there's no magic to this technique, sometimes you can't help but wonder, "How does it know?" The search directory or engine knows by looking at how close to the top of a document and how often a keyword or phrase is mentioned. If you don't get what you want, look at how the list was ranked so you can give better instructions to the search engine the next time.

**Figure 5-10.** You can refine your list of search results in AltaVista by specifying which terms are required or which can be excluded or ignored entirely.

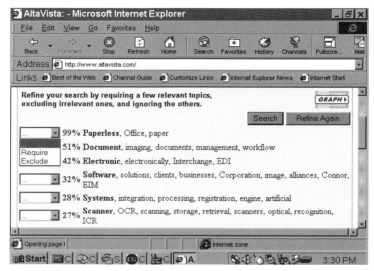

Reprinted with permission of Compaq Corporation.

## Retooling and Refining

Retooling and refining your search are actually two different things. Retooling your search means offering different or adjusted search criteria to search the entire database again. Refining means applying different or adjusted criteria to the subset of results you got this time around (see Figure 5-10).

You will see a button on the search engine screen in close proximity to the keyword search block called refine. It allows you to further hone your results from within the initial set of search results returned.

• *Narrow the search.* Once you've run a search, you'll have some clues as to what to exclude. If you used the phrase *team building* and were hoping for information related to business teams but instead got lots of baseball team information, then you'll want to exclude the word *baseball* by writing "team building – baseball." If what you wanted to build was a baseball team, then typing out "team building" + baseball also narrows the search by demanding the phrase *team building* and the word *baseball* in the result.

• *Broaden the search.* Use a wildcard in the form of an asterisk. The phrase *team build\** would score a hit and return various terms: *team building, builder,* and *builders.* You may also use the Boolean operator OR to broaden your search. For example:

---

**team OR "team building" OR collaboration**

---

In this case you will get documents that contain any of the three terms.

• *Alter your slant.* Changes in word order can change results. The phrase *building teams* will get different results than *team building.*

## Error Messages

If you spend any time searching the Internet, you will encounter error messages. The majority of them relate to mistyped or misspelled URLs. These include:

"Bad Request"

"File Not Found"

"Failed DNS Lookup"

"Host Unknown"

"Host Unavailable"

"Unable to locate host"

"NNTP Server Error"

"Unable to locate the server"

### *URL Spelling*

Check the spelling of the URL. Remember that there should be no spaces in the address line. If you are pulling the address from a document or an e-mail message, use the cut-and-paste technique instead of retyping it. If you are getting the link from a web page, right-mouse click on it and choose Copy Link Location in Netscape (Copy Shortcut in Internet Explorer 4.0) to copy the link to the Windows clipboard for transfer.

### *Put It in Reverse*

An error message may also mean that a particular document you are looking for within a website has disappeared. You can use a technique called backing up. Let's say that the URL you typed in looks like this:

> **www.madeupcompany.com/folderfullofneatstuff/
> documentfullofneatstuff.html**

The document "documentfullofneatstuff.html" no longer exists at that site, and so you get the error message "File not found." Backing up means to back up one slash and then repeat your request. For example:

> **www.madeupcompany.com/folderfullofneatstuff**

If that doesn't work, back up again to the next slash mark and request:

> **www.madeupcompany.com**

Sooner or later you'll hit pay dirt.

It is important to recognize that Internet addresses are changing as we speak. It is very possible that some of the sites referenced in this book have changed addresses or no longer exist. But new sites are also being created every day, so keep searching.

## Security

Security is the next most frequent cause of error messages. Access may be denied based on your system settings, domain name, site restrictions, or absence of a proper password. In these cases you may receive an error message that reads:

"Unauthorized"

"Forbidden"

"Connection refused by host"

"Permission denied"

Remember to always make sure the URL is typed correctly.

## Volume

If the site you are trying to access is unable to take your request because of too much volume, you might receive a message that says:

"Service temporarily overloaded"

"Service unavailable, too many users"

"Network connection was refused by server"

"Too many connections—try again later"

Try clicking on the Reload/Refresh button. If that doesn't work, schedule your request for another time when traffic is lighter.

### Address Change
The site you are trying to access may have moved to a different web address. The message you commonly receive is:

---

> **"The requested URL was not found on this server"**

---

Sites move, appear, and disappear on the Internet all the time. If a site has moved, the owners of the site sometimes leave a forwarding address in the form of a hyperlink to the new location. If they were so rude as to not tell you where they went, use your trusty search engine to hunt them down.

## Learn From This Process for the Next Time

Each time you complete a particularly intricate search, take a moment to note lessons learned. Maybe this was the first time you used Open Text (**www.pinstripe.opentext.com**) and found you could do a positional search (see Figure 5-11). Positional searching means you can request results based on where your keywords appear (e.g., in the title or in the body text). Make a few notes for yourself about what you found useful and what didn't work. Trade information with your office mates. You might even post a tip or add a frequently asked question (FAQ) section on your intranet.

Make sure you are truly searching, not wandering aimlessly. Watch out for the danger signal, which is when you find yourself saying, "That looks interesting, I'll just click on that and then I'll come back." If you make that next click, we'll miss you. I know you started with good intentions. But go just one click too far, and you'll be led from site to site, in a trancelike state, until before you know it the night cleaning crew is dusting your head. You've been there so long they think you are an office fixture.

I've heard people say, "I spent an hour on the Internet, but I couldn't find anything." That tells me they weren't using a well-thought-out

**Figure 5-11.** Open Text is a site that does positional searching. The drop-down menu on the right side of the screen lets you define where in a document you want your search terms to appear. Reprinted with permission.

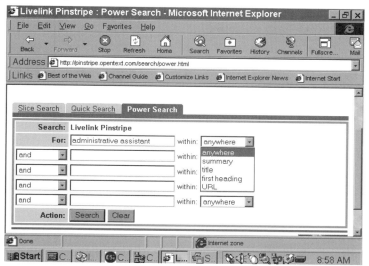

approach to their search. They most likely got on the Net and started to wander. That can be a colossal waste of time. It also means that they didn't use the Internet as their assistant—they used it for distraction or entertainment.

## Tips for Staying Focused

• Keep your successful searching grid (see Figure 5-1) right in front of your nose throughout the search.

• No time to make a grid? Put a self-stick note on your terminal with a focus phrase describing the desired result of your search.

• Consider the source of information you retrieve. Is it a vendor touting its own product or an independent testing lab reporting performance scores? Does the information come from a reputable news source or from someone's personal home page? Don't focus on invalid information.

• Make a bookmark folder for material "that looks interesting," and you can explore it later if you need to.

• Alternatively, keep a separate document in your word processor or make a spreadsheet/database called "that looks interesting" and paste into it URLs you are interested in exploring at another time (an example is given in Chapter 3 in Figure 3-8). This also gives you space to note why or under what circumstances you think the site might be useful, and you can delete it from the list if it hasn't been explored after a time.

• Set an alarm on your computer to remind you when it's time to stop and log off.

## Capturing the Information

Congratulations! You found what you wanted. You need to capture it. How you do that depends on what you want to do with your newfound treasure.

If it's a great site that you'd return to often, you'll want to bookmark it, or make it a shortcut on your desktop screen. You can also print a web page if you have only a temporary need for the information.

## Copyright Approvals

You can copy and paste text and graphics for future use in a document. It is most important, however, to make sure you comply with the appropriate copyright laws. Some organizations will have a page as part of their website that talks about permissions and may even grant them (see Figure 5-12).

Companies may put this information under a link with headings such as "Legal," "Public Relations," "About," or they may use a copyright symbol © at the bottom of the page. In most cases they give an e-mail address or street address to which you can write to get permission to use information. For others, there is a phone number for you to call. If that doesn't work, go to the InterNIC site (**www.internic.net**). This is the Internet Network Information Center, and it provides registry information for

**Figure 5-12.** Microsoft Corp. includes a permissions page on its website pertaining to how to use any software downloaded from its site. Many other websites have similar pages on copy-righted information.

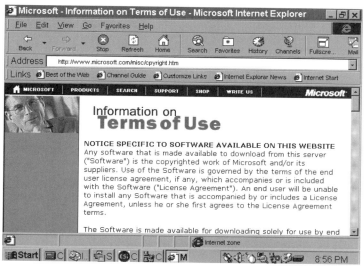

Internet sites. Type in a domain name and you get both a technical and an administrative contact. Your request to use their copyrighted material should go to the administrative contact.

If you complete a search but don't have the time to review the results, save the results page as an HTML document. It is as easy as choosing the pull-down File menu and selecting Save As, then selecting HTML as the Save as file type (see Figure 5-13). You can also add the results page to your Bookmark/Favorites list.

## Downloading

If your treasure is a file, you may be given the opportunity to download it. Downloading is the transferring of a file from another computer to your computer system. Before you ever do your first download, make sure that you have checked your company's computer usage policy. Chances are

**Figure 5-13.** If you don't have time to review all your search results, save the web page as an HTML document so you can read it later, off-line. Make sure you note the directory or folder where you are storing the information so you can find it easily later.

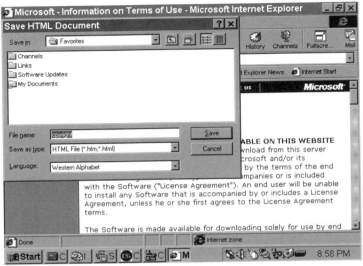

there are regulations about what kind of information you are allowed to download.

Hyperlinks serve as the key to most downloadable files. The link will say, "Click here to download the latest version of the xyz file."

If you click on the link to start a download, you may be presented with the choice to either open the file or save it to disk (see Figure 5-14). The general recommendation is to always err on the side of safety and save to an external disk. Create a folder with a name specific to the use of the file and then store it there. If you dump everything into a folder marked download it may be hard to establish what's what. Your system administrator may have reserved a location on your corporate system for those files.

Downloaded files will often have extensions such as .DOC or .TXT (word processing), .GIF or .JPG (graphics), and .WAV (music). If the file

**Figure 5-14.** Open file or save to disk? That is the question when downloading a file. Save it to disk if possible. Your browser software may have a folder set up for Downloads, but it is better to give the folder a specific name so you can easily retrieve it later.

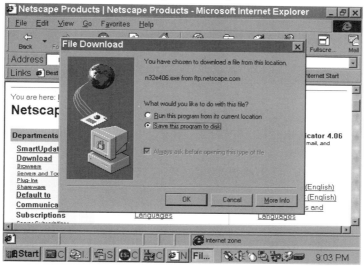

extension is .EXE, it is the executable file of a program. To run the program, double left click on the file. If, however, you see the extension .ZIP, the file has been compressed. Most systems have an "unzip" program loaded to automatically uncompress .ZIP files. Double clicking on the file while within the unzip program is all you'll need to do in most cases.

## Tips and Strategies

In downloading software updates, you can expect to be presented with a choice of sites from which you can download a particular file (see Figure 5-15). You might base your choice on which location is geographically closer to you. A better strategy is to choose the site in a time zone that's likely to be experiencing less traffic. Late afternoon and evening hours are usually high-traffic hours on the Net, and your download will take longer.

**Figure 5-15.** When presented with a list of download sites to choose from, pick a location that's in a time zone with less traffic. If you are online in New York at 4:00 pm, you might want to try the California download site instead.

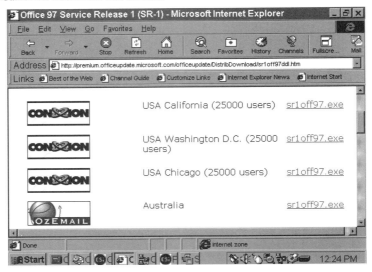

**Figure 5-16.** Presenters University has a library of graphics and templates for your use. Most are free. Some do have a fee attached and will tell you.

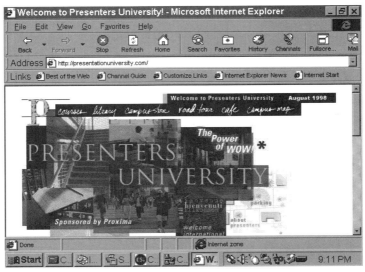

Reprinted with permission of Proxima Corproration.

## Graphics

If you see a graphic on a web page you want to capture, right-mouse click on the graphic and choose from the pop-up menu Save Image/Picture As, then fill in the blanks in the Save As dialog box and give it a name. If you want help in creating presentations, go to Presenters University (**www.pre-sentersuniversity.com**). There you'll find advice and a library of graphics and templates you can use (see Figure 5-16).

If you want to search the Web for a specific image, go to AltaVista (**www.altavista.com**) and use the syntax "image :" whenever you want a picture of something (see Figure 5-17). For example, want a picture of a phone? Type in:

**image : phone**

Want a Motorola phone? Then use:

**image : phone +motorola**

Other sources for images and graphics are:

Yahoo!                (**www.yahoo.com**/Computers_and_Internet/Multimedia/Pictures**)

Chankstore Fonts    (**www.chank.com**) for font and typeface designs

**Figure 5-17.** Searching for pictures at AltaVista is simple as long as you use the correct syntax. This is a search results list for the term

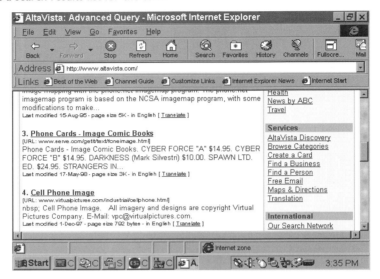

## Templates

One of the best uses of downloading is to retrieve templates. Very often the software manufacturer has developed templates that you can use so you don't have to reinvent the wheel. If you use Microsoft Office, for example, you are in luck. Go to the Microsoft home page, find the software product you are interested in, and you will find a library of templates, wizards, and add-ins available for download. Microsoft has built this connection into each of its programs. Go to the Help menu and click on Microsoft on the Web (see Figure 5-18). You don't even have to type in an address.

CCH Business Owner's Toolkit (**www.toolkit.cch.com**) is a terrific resource for templates, forms, and other business documents that you can download and use at no charge (see Figure 5-19). You don't need to be a business owner to make use of this site.

**Figure 5-18.** Microsoft on the Web can be accessed through the pull-down Help menu of any Microsoft Office product.

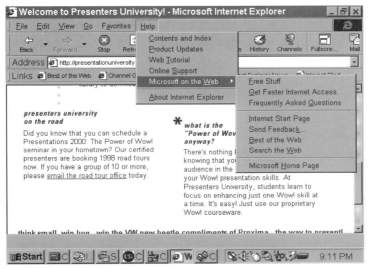

Reprinted with permission of Proxima Corproration.

**Figure 5-19.** Need a job requirements checklist or a business plan model? CCH offers a variety of free, downloadable forms and templates.

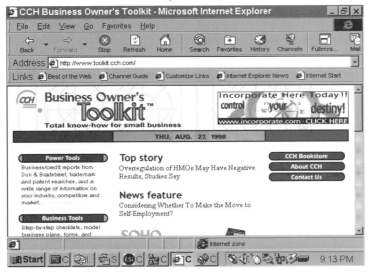

Reprinted with permission of CCH Incorporated.

If you are using a screen saver, turn it off before starting to capture information or files. A screen saver can interrupt or interfere with a download. To turn off a Windows 95 screen saver, right-mouse click anywhere on your Windows 95 desktop and choose Properties. A new dialog box appears. Select the Screen Saver tab and change the screen saver selection to None using the drop-down menu.

Chapter 6

# The Inside Scoop: Using Your Company Intranet

Here's a recipe. Take one Internet. Wash in hot water, dry on the high heat setting. Voilà! You have an intranet. Simplistic, yes, but think of an intranet as a "shrunk down" Internet. By using the intranet as your assistant, you can have fast and easy access to information inside your organization as well.

In this chapter we'll explore the differences between the Internet and an intranet (or internal network). You will see how an intranet grows and develops in an organization and how to use it to close information gaps.

Intranets are becoming lands of opportunity for administrative professionals. At the end of this chapter we'll explore your new role in this dynamic information management system.

## Internet vs. Intranet

An intranet is an internal network that uses the same set of protocols, TCP/IP, that the Web does. So you can use your browser software to navigate through information that's stored on an intranet. It offers potentially the same resources as the Internet with three major differences:

1. *Security.* Access to the intranet is afforded only to company employees as the company sees fit.

2. *Selective information.* An intranet contains only the information your company chooses to post on it. Unlike the Internet, no one can post to it indiscriminately.

3. *Structure.* The company can impose any organizational structure it chooses, whereas the Internet has no structure.

## Examples of Intranet Usage

In the classes I teach, students have given me many examples of how their companies makes use of an intranet.

### Personnel Records

A common application is to do personnel record changes on the intranet. You can change your payroll deductions, benefits choices, and savings plan investments. You would most likely be given a personal identification number that gives you access to your records automatically. Within forty-eight hours you receive a message that lets you know that the changes have taken effect.

**Figure 6-1.** A skills matrix can be kept on the company's human resources intranet to help project managers quickly identify potential employees for the job.

| Name | Team Building | Communication | ISO 9000 | Excel |
|------|---------------|---------------|----------|-------|
| D.H. | X | X | | X |
| B.J. | | | X | X |

Companies that run major projects keep an employee skills matrix online (see Figure 6-1) maintained by human resources. You can quickly match the skills you require with available employees.

## Travel

Many companies have access to their in-house travel department or outside agency online. You can request to have airline tickets delivered either to the office or to your home and input other information on-screen, such as the days and time of departure. The travel office sends you electronically all the flight options (including prices); you pick your flight and your tickets are automatically printed and delivered by the next business day before noon.

## Services

Some companies allow you to order your prescription medications through the insurance plan and have them delivered to your office or home. The information you need to enter is the prescription number and the physician name.

You'll see everything from floor plans, social notices, policy statements, new forms, ongoing projects, requests for help, lessons learned, how-to's and what-if's, and self-paced learning curriculum on a company intranet.

## Online Meetings

Discussion groups are formed to post messages about company issues, competitive products, trials of new products, ideas for shortcuts, software tips and tricks, FAQs, and kudos for coworkers. New employee information, child care information, van pools, you name it—it's probably on a company intranet.

Some companies with widespread locations may use chat rooms to host online meetings. The costs can be less than face-to-face meetings, videoconferencing, or even teleconferencing. Online chat sessions work best when there would be little conflict about the issues at hand, the group can work collaboratively, and everybody can type fast. This is a perfect forum for your administrative council or network to chat once a week on issues, current topics, and problem solving.

You can use Microsoft Net Meeting or Netscape's Conference to set up an online meeting. Your system administrator may already have this software set up and ready to go. These systems allow you to connect directly to other employees in a chat room–like atmosphere. The system also allows you to have a drawing board opened at the same time so that people can "brainstorm" during a meeting and exchange files as well as ideas. You can hold meetings via an audio/video connection or just by using the computer keyboard like you do in a chat room. You can look in a directory and see who is hooked up, call in to any meeting (if the host permits you in), and connect automatically.

## The Growth of an Intranet

The main purpose of an intranet should be to eliminate information obstacles. These are things that get in the way of doing business effectively and efficiently. They fall into three categories:

1. Obstacles to finding and transferring information (gaps)

2. Obstacles to collaboration

3. Obstacles to translating information into usable knowledge

## The Development Path

The path of development of a company intranet will usually follow stages aligned with addressing one and/or more of these three obstacles. Most often, a company will form an intranet in a effort to go paperless. It will start to put things such as phone lists and employee newsletters into a common electronic space. Immediate growth usually takes place in the area of announcements (e.g., new policies and procedures).

Many human resources departments were the first kids on the block to use intranet technology because so much of their process was enhanced by the use of this tool. Pretty soon, the realization sets in companywide that it is much more cost-effective to handle documents electronically than it is to publish and distribute them on paper, and the race to the intranet is on.

Not only does the number of documents increase, but the usage of the system does as well. As people integrate this tool into their culture, they think of more ways in which to use it. You will not only see the list of available training classes, for example, but reviews of each class submitted by attendees, copies of the course materials, online registration for the classes, and online discussion groups to continue the learning process.

## Closing Information Gaps

Anytime you see an information "gap," start thinking intranet. A "gap" is present when there is lag time between the request for information and its delivery. Here are some examples:

"I'll need to look that up."

"Let me get back to you on that."

"I wouldn't even know where to start looking for that!"

### *Lag Time Gaps*

Are you "information central"? Unless the request is so unusual that it's a once-in-a-lifetime occurrence, you might want to close the lag time gap between the requester and the information by posting it for electronic access. If on more than one occasion you have been tempted to deck your coworkers because they asked you to interrupt your high-value work to clear a jam on the printer, a diagram showing the fix online might be helpful. Take the time to evaluate the requests you get and how an intranet could handle them for you. Create a grid that will help you see patterns. Figure 6-2 is a sample grid. List the request and then check off any columns that apply. For example:

• *Information transfer.* A check in this column indicates this is a case of pure information exchange, passing information from its source back to the requester. No formatting or repackaging is required.

• *Can be stored publicly.* Check this box if confidentiality is not an issue. Is there any reason why the information could not be stored publicly? A good indicator is when you hear yourself muttering under your breath, "Why didn't they just look it up themselves?" If you post this kind of infor-

**Figure 6-2.** Use a simple grid, like this example, to categorize common information requests. Many requests are for information that can easily be made public on an intranet, saving everyone loads of time.

| Request | Information transfer | Can be stored publicly | Requires no judgment or expertise | Repeat request |
|---|---|---|---|---|
| "Where do we store the blank transparencies?" | X | X | X | X |
| "I need a conference room for Thursday afternoon." | X | X | X | X |
| "Get me John Doe's personnel record." | X | | X | |

mation on an intranet, access may be so easy that they will be able to look it up for themselves.

• *Requires no judgment or expertise.* Did you have to analyze the information or filter it? If you did nothing to enhance the value of this information, then place a check here.

• *Repeat request.* "They've asked me this a hundred times. If they ask me that one more time, I'll scream." Let's not make it 101, and save your throat, to boot. Repeat questions indicate that people need a piece of information frequently, but they don't know or understand how to get what they need. HR departments, for example, are charged with putting out new benefits packages. They will immediately see that 80 percent of the questions they get from employees relate to 20 percent of the policy. That's the place where people need more support, a clearer explanation, and a simplified form. Good HR departments don't keep answering the same question over and over; they fix the confusing parts.

After two weeks of keeping this grid, you should have a clear picture of which information you want to automate. Look for requests that have checks in all four columns of the grid. These represent low-value work for you. You are not contributing your expertise or judgment; you are acting as a conduit. With so many high-value requests waiting for your attention, shouldn't you delegate these low-value ones to your assistant? Some administrators will say, "People will still come and ask me. They think it's easier." If you make it easier for them to go to the intranet, they'll do that.

When deciding to post information to an intranet, make sure that you consider these questions:

- Does my solution help us do this task better, faster, cheaper?

- Will my solution cause a problem for others involved in this process?

- Will I be meeting a business need by posting this information?

### Time Zone Gaps

A different type of "gap" you might address is the time zone factor. If you work in the New York office and you have to wait until the San Francisco office opens to get access to the required data, an intranet gives you that access twenty-four hours a day.

## Land of Opportunity

Intranets are a perfect place to show off the expertise and brilliance of administrative professionals. One of the major roles you play is that of liaison. A term originating in French cooking, a liaison is something that is used to cause two ingredients that don't usually mix to do so. As your intranet grows, so do the opportunities for you to develop ways to bring people together with information to produce results. You can set up virtual teams in chat rooms, float documents onto the intranet for group editing and discussion, and link remote locations together almost seamlessly. Folks can see work in progress and streamline their work process through electronic collaboration.

Start looking for ways your organization could use this tool to save time, effort, and money. An immediate example comes to mind when your company has different types of computers running different operating systems, all needing access to central information. The question becomes, "Why not use the intranet?"

The next level of sophistication comes when the intranet is used as the vehicle that adds value to the information housed there.

## Enterprise Reporting

You may have heard a term called enterprise reporting. It means electronically storing, enhancing, and managing the information your company uses to make decisions—your intellectual capital.

Let me give you an example: Without these electronic tools, it might be necessary for you to collect sales results from each salesperson in your department, then tabulate the results into a monthly sales report. On the third of each month (provided everyone turned their stuff in to you on time), each department manager would get a complete copy of their own report and every other department's report as well. Part of the manager's time, or yours, would be spent sifting through the report for data that's relevant to them. After you install an intranet, the documents can be stored and transmitted electronically. While the intranet's immediate benefit is that it saves paper, the "treasure hunt" process each manager has to go through to find relevant information may still be necessary.

Today, the paradigm is different. Enterprise reporting allows the information to be structured and stored in a way for managers of the business to pull only and exactly the information they need. They can structure a "report" based on the information they need to run their part of the business. They can view top-level information or drill-down for more detail. Information is updated as it happens. If an order for a product is entered into the system, that entry also updates the sales figures. Therefore the information is real-time and dynamic, allowing for more accurate decision making.

Enterprise reporting allows the capture of information as a part of doing business. In all areas of the business the system monitors daily transactions of data exchange and allows you to build a knowledge base with that information.

That paradigm shift applies to more than just the mechanics of how the data is managed. It extends to the people running the business as well. Previously, a manager could count on being inundated with reports, but could find useful information as a result of hunting. For some, this was a passive activity, somewhat like shopping with the "I'll know it when I see it" philosophy. Using enterprise reporting on an intranet, you need to know what you want to see. You are making specific queries, much like searching on the Internet.

## Funneling and Filtering

The good news is that funneling and filtering information is your administrative strong suit from the word go. Your job has always required you to focus on high-value information and enhance it even more. What a perfect match! As intranets grow, so do your opportunities to control and contribute to that growth. This is a perfect opportunity to use your skill and expertise to take the lead in building your company intranet.

## Home Pages

The subject of building a web page is a book unto itself. In fact, there are some good ones on the market ready and waiting for you. If you don't know how to build a web page, ask your system administrator. It may be as simple as doing a document in your word processor and saving it in HTML format. Microsoft Office 97 can do this for you just by changing the file type in the Save As dialog box. If it's not that easy in your system, take a class, get that book, find a mentor, or try a web page software package such as Microsoft's FrontPage.

Once again, let the Internet be your assistant. An online tutorial that is designed for beginners can be found at **www.w3-tech.com/crash/HTML Menu.html**. You can do it! You may find a whole new aspect of your profession opening up as a result of this electronic way of life. You could be the webmaster!

## *Department*

To start, set up a home page for your department (see Figure 6-3). Take some time to brainstorm and keep track of requests your department gets from your internal customers. What information could you post

**Figure 6-3**
A mockup design of a web page for your department.

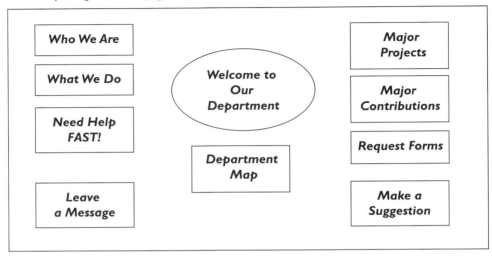

that would help them do business with you more easily? What information do you need from them so you can assist them most efficiently?
Post those questions on a welcome page, or link to a service request
form.

Think about the companies that you do business with on the Net.
Which ones are your favorites? What do you like most about using their
home page? One of my current favorites is Amazon.com (**www.amazon.
com**). First of all, I love the fact that I don't have to buy music from a person half my age who says to me, "Mozart? What band does he play with?"
That notwithstanding, I like this online bookseller's home page because I
don't have to scroll down pages and pages to do a product search; it's
right up-front. They remember me, so once my profile is in their system, I
can choose to buy any book or record with just a single click. No long fill-
in-the-blank forms asking for information I filled in the last time; I just
click. I also like that the Amazon.com website is very intuitive, as if they
know what I'm thinking. Even though I can purchase with one click, right
underneath that click spot it tells me I can undo it if I want to. They con-
firm my order and its shipment with a courteous e-mail message. Though

this may sound foolish, here goes: They seem like smart businesspeople, and they are nice, to boot. They appear genuinely concerned about meeting my needs and making me happy. I've obviously never met them, so the only way I could have gotten this impression is from their website. You're right, it does sound foolish, but I like doing business with nice, smart people, don't you?

Don't forget to consider your least favorite sites as well. What is it you don't like about them? What about the design of the page makes it hard to do business with them? It's a valuable model to help you avoid pitfalls in designing your own page.

## Boss

Another opportunity is to build a start page or home page for your boss (see Figure 6-4). Include links to all the boss's favorite sites organized according to a priority list. You may want a link to your company's stock price, and the prices of your top three competitors. The boss may want to see abstracts of articles mentioning your company in the financial news, as well as links to the sales figures by region and materials cost reports.

**Figure 6-4**
A mockup design for a web page for your boss.

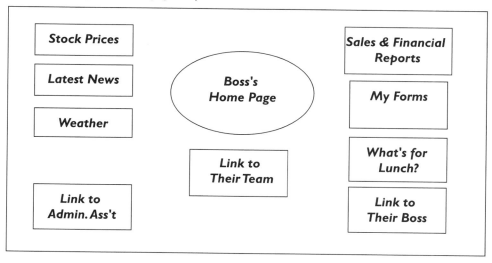

The boss might even want today's cafeteria menu. I don't know what your boss wants, but you do.

### Administrative Team

Think about doing a home page for the administrative assistants. Put links to the top-ten most requested electronic forms, the procedures manual, and frequently used vendors (e.g., online office supplies, overnight shipping, computer repair). Post FAQs and their answers, along with tips for using company software most effectively. This is also a great place to post templates and presentation graphics for all to share.

Let me leave you with one more intranet example. A client company of mine has turned its company cafeteria into a profit center. It not only serves breakfast and lunch, but caters meetings, sells fully cooked and packaged dinners to go, and even has a small grocery store attached. You can order food or groceries over the company intranet to take home with you. Your order has to be made before 3:00 P.M. so they can be waiting for you at the garage exit when you are ready to leave. Working late? Send an e-mail and they'll store your order for you until you're ready. Now that's using your intranet!

# Chapter 7

# Letting Your New Assistant Take Charge

Are you ready for some adventure? In the introduction of this book I outlined some of the typical tasks that you as an administrative professional might be asked to do. In this chapter, I'll show you several ways to accomplish each one of them using the Internet as your assistant.

Websites change without notice. By the time you read this book a site may have changed; there will most likely be a pointer, like a forwarding address, to tell you how to find it.

Your best resource is other administrative professionals trying to accomplish the same kinds of tasks you are. Ask them what sites they use. Be prepared to offer your favorites in return.

## "Get Me Information On . . ."

The resources you need to find information on the Net are covered in Chapter 3. Chapter 5 covers the logic to use when searching.

**Figure 7-1.** A search grid clarifies your strategy for finding targeted information—in this case, finding consultants to create a paperless office.

| |
|---|
| **Define the target:**<br>Find a consultant.<br><br>**Define success:**<br>Three consultants recommended for their successful implementations in companies like ours. |
| **How will this information be used?**<br>Give to purchasing department to add to our supplier list. |
| **Keywords:**<br>　**Include:**<br>Paperless, office automation, online forms, intranet, implementation<br><br>　**Exclude:**<br>Sales force |
| **Word strings or phrases:**<br>"Going paperless" "paperless office" "office automation" "online forms" "online documents" |
| **Query/request structure**<br>Office automation +consultant  paperless NEAR implementation<br>"paperless office" Near consultant |
| **Preferred tools:** AltaVista, Infoseek,  Ask Jeeves |

Let's pretend your boss has been considering taking your office paperless. The boss asks you to "find out about it." Pull out your trusty search grid and begin formulating your search strategy. Start with a clear explanation of what information is desired (see Figure 7-1). Going paperless is a huge topic, so you'll want to get clarity about what a successful search result actually will look like.

The All Business Network (**www.all-biz.com**) is jam-packed with business-related sites—travel, business books, and online publications, just to name a few. Another wonderful site for administrative professionals to use is Cybercraft (**www.cybercraft.net**). The site was originally built for executives, but the site developer realized that administrative partners were using it as well and started tailoring it accordingly. Explore the left-hand side of the Cybercraft home page (see Figure 7-2) for links to all the major

**Figure 7-2.** Cybercraft is truly a one-stop shopping site with valuable links for business executives and administrative partners.

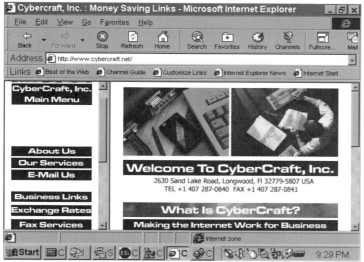

Reprinted with permission.

shipping companies; you'll even find screens to estimate shipping costs and delivery dates. You'll find links to all the U.S. government sites you could ever wish for. A link to the National Speakers Association gives hints on building presentations, as well as access to anecdotes and quotations. This developer really did his homework. There are not many sites I would recommend you wander through, but this is one-stop shopping and worth the trip.

Try my two favorite sites for business research as well. The first is @Brint (**www.brint.com**). This site is devoted totally to business research. The index is very focused and hard to beat (see Figure 7-3).

A second choice is the American Management Association (**www. amanet.org**), which houses a wealth of business knowledge in its Information Resource Center (see Figure 7-4).

**Figure 7-3.** @Brint is devoted entirely to business research, and its index is hard to beat.

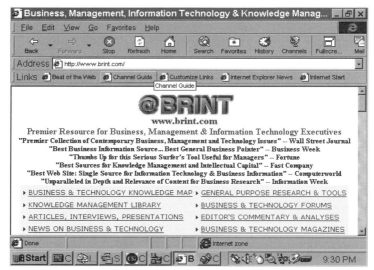

Reprinted with permission of @Brint Research Institute.

**Figure 7-4.** The AMA's Information Resource Center houses a wealth of business information but is accessible for free only to AMA members.

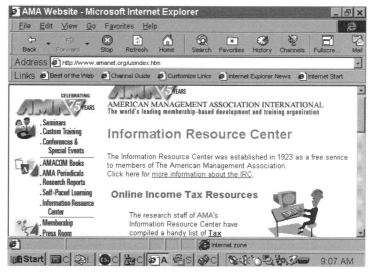

**Figure 7-5.** BizTravel is an award-winning site that chooses travel options for you based on your preferences.

Reprinted with permission of BizTravel.

## "Book My Trip to . . ."

Booking travel is a wonderful example of a task best done on the Internet. Although travel agents are terrific folks, I find that calling the travel agent, getting different options, going back to clear them with the boss, calling back to book the tickets, sitting on hold, and so on is too long and involved a process. Faxing and e-mailing the information is not much of an improvement. Of course, by then the meeting is changed and all bets are off, and you're back to square one.

If you book business travel, a good site to use is BizTravel. This award-winning site is simple, straightforward, and powerful (see Figure 7-5). The user profile that you fill in when you first visit the site allows you to state preferences as to specific airlines and whether to choose flights based first on schedule, then on price. They make an effort to help you meet your travel goals (e.g., collecting mileage for a free ticket) by asking you a series of questions and then choosing travel options based on your preferences. Based on your requested dates, times, and destinations, BizTravel will create a recommended itinerary with all other options available. Print that list for your boss's briefcase so that if she needs another option while traveling, the information is at her fingertips. She'll have no need to call the travel agent or to lug an OAG (Official Airline Guide).

One of the features I like best about BizTravel is the calendar transfer feature. Once the itinerary is set, I can drag and drop those items from my browser window onto my schedule in Outlook 98. No cutting, pasting, or retyping is required, and that's how electronic organization should work. Check the site for the list of scheduling software supported.

Another travel site to try is The Trip. This site has a feature called FlightTracker that provides you with flight departure and arrival times, gates, and other information (see Figure 7-6).

Internet Travel Network (**www.itn.com**) offers seat selection and driving directions with maps to and from the airport. You can also search for the flight with the best seat available if that is your more important criteria (see Figure 7-7).

Even if you don't book travel for your boss, having these options on hand is still a plus. If you deal with an in-house travel agent, use the Internet for gathering information on possible choices, then use the agent to help with ticketing and changes.

If price is the first concern, consider using IntelliTrip (**www.intellitrip.com**). This is a metasearch engine keyed to search for low-price airfares (see Figure 7-8).

If you are booking international travel you might find one-stop shopping sites such as Travelocity (**www.travelocity.com**) or Microsoft Expedia (**www.expedia.msn.com**) to be your best bet. They will allow you to book your travel, plus they offer currency converters, weather reports, maps, and city guides.

The Internet Travel Network (**www.itn.net**) and American Express Travel (**www.americanexpress.com/travel**) bring you access both to information on the Net and links to travel agencies. TravelWeb (**www.travelweb.com**) (see

**Figure 7-6.** FlightTracker is a service your company's frequent flyers may want to subscribe to for tracking domestic flight schedules.

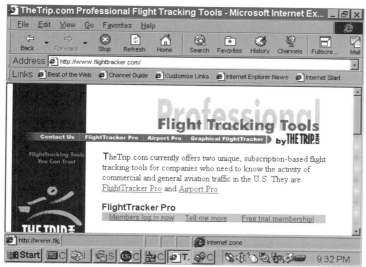

Reprinted with permission of TheTrip.com.

**Figure 7-7.** The Internet Travel Network will help you find your way to and from any airport.

Reprinted with permission of ITN.

**Figure 7-8.** IntelliTrip's focus is finding you the lowest airfare.

Reprinted with permission of TheTrip.com.

**Figure 7-9.** Travel Web's main feature is its thorough hotel search.

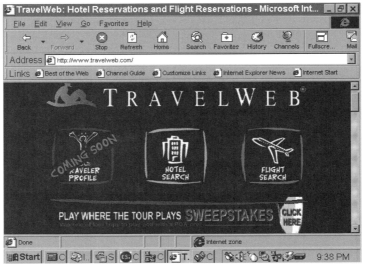

Reprinted with permission of TravelWeb.

Figure 7-9) offers hotel and resort booking for 18,000 properties worldwide. You can search for a hotel with the features you prefer (e.g., in-room workstation, gymnasium).

### *Information to Know: Business Travel Websites*

| | |
|---|---|
| BizTravel | **www.biztravel.com** |
| The Trip | **www.thetrip.com** |
| Internet Travel Network | **www.itn.com** |
| Travelocity | **www.travelocity.com** |
| Microsoft Expedia | **www.expedia.msn.com** |
| IntelliTrip | **www.intellitrip.com** |
| American Express Travel | **www.americanexpress.com/travel** |
| TravelWeb | **www.travelweb.com** |

## *Other Travel-Related Sites of Interest*

### *Currency*

- To buy foreign currency before you leave home, try Direct FX (**www.foreign-currency.com**) and it will "show you the money."

- Need to find the nearest ATM when you get to your destination? Look at Visa-ATM Locator (**www.visa.com/cgi-bin/vee/pd/atm/main.html**) or MasterCard/Cirrus ATM Locator (**www.master card.com/atm**).

- What's the right amount to tip? Visit **www.cis.columbia.edu/homepages/gonzalu/tipping.html**.

### Legal Advice

- Didn't tip enough? Get overseas judicial assistance from the U.S. Department of State (**www.travel.state.gov/judicial_assistance.html**). This site lists U.S. Consulates and can also assist with passports, visas, and travel advisories and warnings.

### Cultural Barriers

- "How do you say...?" Listen to audio clips of common phrases in forty-four languages (**www.travlang.com**).

- Business and cultural information to study before you begin your travels is available at **www.getcustoms.com**.

### Health

- Looking for tips on staying healthy when abroad? The U.S. Centers for Disease Control can help (**www.cdc.gov/travel/travel.html**).

### Security Subscription Services

- Air Security International (**www.airsecurity.com**)

- Pinkerton's (**www.pinkertons.com**)

### Booking Off-Site Meeting Rooms

If you are asked to book meeting space along with the travel, go to AltaVista (**www.altavista.com**) and search for:

```
         city name +hotels +"meeting rooms"
```

**Figure 7-10.** If your company has a corporate account with a hotel chain such as Hyatt, try its home page for information on scheduling a meeting room.

Reprinted with permission of Hyatt Hotels Corporation.

You could also try:

city name +"convention bureau"

Convention Central Information Services (**www.conventioncentral.com**) is another useful site.

If you know you want to book a room at a Hyatt Hotel because your company has a corporate contract, you can go to the Hyatt website (**www.hyatt.com**), pick your city, then select the section labeled banquets (see Figure 7-10).

The search engine AskJeeves (**www.askjeeves.com**) also works well for locating a meeting room (see Figure 7-11) because it prompts you to construct simple questions in plain English instead of Boolean search terms. Try search terms such as:

---

**book banquet room in Pittsburgh**

---

### "Find the Specs on Our Competitor's Product"

You might think that it would be too easy to be able to go to your competitor's website and pull the information you require. You're right, and that's probably the best place to start. Many companies put product specifications online to better educate and inform their customer. If you don't know the competitor's website, try "**www.companyname.com**," typing in the actual company name as you know it (e.g., **www.microsoft.com**). If that doesn't take you where you want to go, try the initials of the company (e.g., **www.att.com**).

A different route might be to look for a newsgroup for users of the product. Use Deja News (**www.dejanews.com**) to find the group you need. Post your questions about the product and see what messages post in reply. You can also use Tile.net (**www.tile.net**) to get statistics on a newsgroup (e.g., actual readers of the group, number of messages per day) to narrow your choices of newsgroups even further.

A third choice is to use a search engine that searches USENET. Choose USENET on the list or drop-down search menu of one of the major search engines (see Figure 7-12). The results you get back will include hyperlinks to each posting that fits your criteria.

Another tactic is to contact a vendor who stocks the product you are interested in. If it is a product that is sold by merchants online, they may have pictures and specifications posted on their own websites. Go to the AskJeeves site (**www.askjeeves.com**) and ask, "Where can I

**Figure 7-11.** The AskJeeves website with its natural language interface is useful for locating to-the-point information such as hotels with banquet facilities.

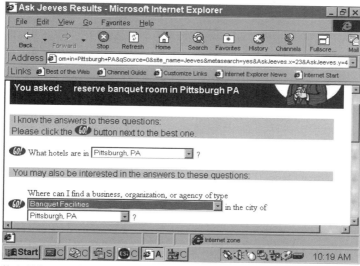

**Figure 7-12.** Among its search capabilities, AltaVista lets you search USENET newsgroups through a link at the right-hand side of the screen.

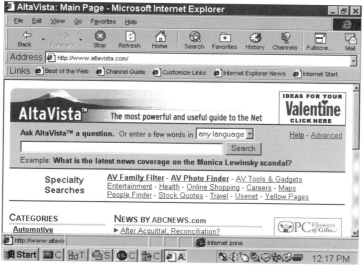

**Figure 7-13.** NewsBot, a news channel of the HotBot search engine, searches recent business news articles across a range of industry publications and can search for pictures too.

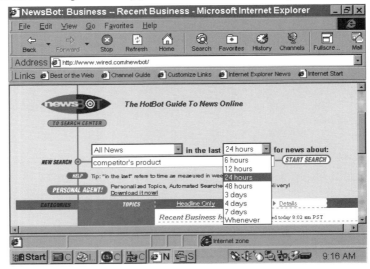

buy [product name]?" Then search that vendor's site for the product information.

Yet another alternative is to search industry publications. NewsBot (**www.wired.com/newbot**) is a business news resource that you can search for reviews and pictures of the product (see Figure 7-13).

Try the site hosted by Michigan State University's Center for International Business Education and Research (**http://ciber.bus.msu.edu/busres.htm**). This is a terrific resource if your competitor does business internationally.

## "Where's That Package?"

The folks at FedEx must be very creative people. The company introduced itself to the marketplace offering a service that no one really knew they

**Figure 7-14.** At the FedEx website, customers can track the status of their shipments even without the intervention of customer service.

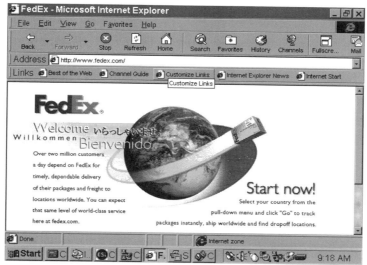

needed. What a paradigm shift that was! But FedEx didn't stop there. It took the concept of the Internet one step further and developed an **extranet** so that not only employees but customers could have access to information about the transport process, but so do customers (see Figure 7-14). Not to say the customer service folks weren't doing a great job, but it must have dawned on someone, "Why have a middleman?" FedEx customers are smart cookies. By making that information available directly to customers, and FedEx customer service folks can concentrate on bigger and better things.

What was once revolutionary is standard today. You can search for the status of your shipment with most major companies as long as you have the necessary data, such as the tracking number and the date shipped.

**Figure 7-15.** Smart Ship will tell you who has the best rate for sending your packages.

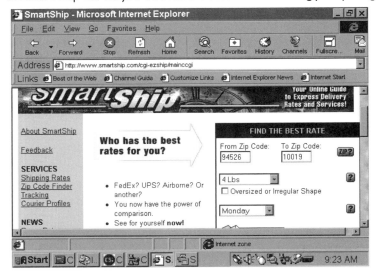

Reprinted with permission of Virtran, Inc.

Other domestic and international shippers are represented online as well. One unique site is Smart Ship (see Figure 7-15), which gives you comparative shipping rates if you are looking for the cheapest and fastest way to go.

### *Information to Know:*
### *Domestic/International Shippers Online*

FedEx                        **www.fedex.com**

U.S. Postal Service          **www.usps.com**

United Parcel Service        **www.ups.com**

**Figure 7-16.** *The New York Times* online has all the news that's fit to digitize, although some content is available by subscription only.

Reprinted by permission. Copyright © 1998 The New York Times Company.

DHL                     **www.dhl.com**

Smart Ship              **www.smartship.com**

## "There's an Article in the *Times* I Need to See"

This is too easy. Ready? If it's *The New York Times*, use **www.nytimes.com** (see Figure 7-16). If it's the *L.A. Times*, you guessed it—**www.latimes.com**. If it's in the "city too small to be on the map *Times*," then you'll have to look further.

Your first try could be "**www.nameofpaper.com**," since many publications are now online. You can also search by news topic and time frame in NewsBot (**www.wired.com/newbot**) or simply try your trusty favorite search engine.

**Figure 7-17.** *Dow Jones Interactive* lets subscribers browse various news and database services and has a push service for customizable news.

Reprinted with permission of Dow Jones Interactive.

If you don't mind the subscription fee, Dow Jones Interactive (**www.djinteractive.com**) has several user-friendly services to choose from that offer a wide range of significant business content—from the top news of the day to breaking news to in-depth background information on numerous companies, industries, or newsworthy persons (see Figure 7-17).

## "I Need Directions and a Map to . . ."

Psychologists and comedians tell us that men don't like to ask for directions, they like maps. According to these folks, women don't like to have maps, they like directions. Lucky for you, you can have both.

Many sites including Excite, Yahoo!, Infoseek, and Lycos link to the MapQuest site (**www.mapquest.com**), where you can get maps and direc-

**Figure 7-18.** Interactive maps at MapQuest will give you directions for your long-distance road trips.

Reprinted with permission of MapSys, Inc.

tions for long-distance trips and even some local ones, too (see Figure 7-18). MapsonUs (**www.mapsonus.com**) is also a strong site, and its printed maps are top quality. To test mapping software, see if it can find your address and give accurate driving directions home from your office. (Of course, if you feel as if you live at your office, pick another test route.)

There are other useful websites for preparing for a road trip as well:

- AutoPilot (**www.freetrip.com**) gives you up to three routes to choose from. This can be of value if you run into a delay on the highway and want to reroute (see Figure 7-19).

- Expedia Maps (**www.expediamaps.com/drivingdirections.asp**) lets you use hotels and airports as start and end points (see Figure 7-20). The best part is that you don't have to know their specific street address.

**Figure 7-19.** AutoPilot lets you select up to three alternative routes to your destination so you are prepared if you want to beat traffic.

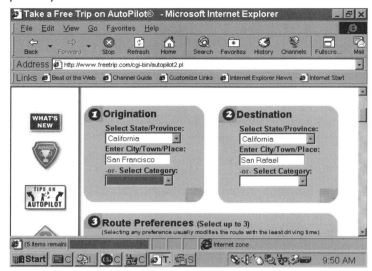

Reprinted with permission of MapSys Inc.

**Figure 7-20.** Expedia Maps is a service created by the Microsoft Network.

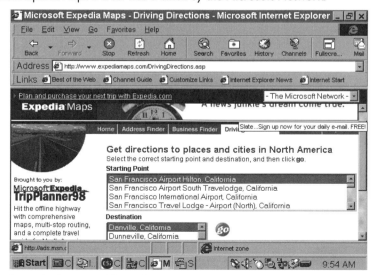

Reprinted with permision of Compaq Corporation.

**Figure 7-21.** Road Watch America (RWA) Direct is a nationwide service.

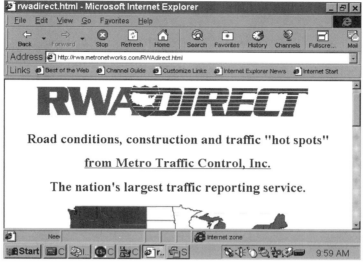

Reprinted with permission of RWA.

• When the boss says, "I need the nearest dry cleaners" or whatever other service, point your browser to Yahoo Maps (**www.maps.yahoo.com**). Enter an address in the vicinity you'll be in, and you'll get a map and local business directory. You can also get driving directions.

• Road Watch America Direct (**www.rwa.metronetworks.com/rwa direct.html**) gives traffic reports and road conditions all over the U.S. (see Figure 7-21).

• My favorite driving site is **www.speedtrap.com.** The name is self-explanatory. It gives me a heads-up on the location and appearance of highway speed traps. (As always, I want to be a courteous, law-abiding guest in the state I am visiting.)

## "Get Theater Tickets for My Client and Me the Night of . . ."

Playbill Online (**www.playbill.com**) lists theaters in more than 100 cities (see Figure 7-22). Some theaters even make the seating charts and performance reviews available.

If you are trying to get tickets to a well-known (or long-run) theater production, it may have its own website from which you can order tickets directly. Cirque du Soleil has its own website listing cities in which the show is playing, performance schedules, and a ticket order form.

Another possibility is to try a search directory such as Yahoo! or Excite and use this search string (don't forget the spaces before each plus sign):

> *"name of show in quotes"* +tickets +city

If you have a preferred ticket vendor—Ticketmaster, Telecharge, or Bass, for example—you can try their online sites. Depending on the city, Sidewalk (**www.sidewalk.com**) city guides might be the place to go to check theater schedules and other events (see Figure 7-23).

Theater-Central (**www.theater-central.com**) will tell you what's happening on the New York Broadway stage. And if all else fails, MovieLink (**www.movielink.com**) will show you what's playing at the picture show—and even let you buy the movie tickets in advance.

If your boss is going out of town, the best bet to get theater information and performance schedules might be to e-mail the concierge at the hotel where the boss will be staying. Ask for an e-mail confirmation back from the hotel with directions to the theater and local restaurant recommendations to add to the boss's travel folder.

## "Find Out What Our Customers Are Saying About Our New Product"

Newsgroups and discussion groups are tailor-made for this type of request. Deja News (**www.dejanews.com**) is a good resource for locating the group

**Figure 7-22.** Playbill Online caters to the theater crowd both on the Great White Way and regionally.

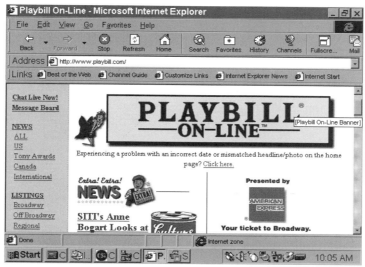

Reprinted with permission of playbill.com.

**Figure 7-23.** Many major cities are served by Sidewalk, Microsoft's city guides on the Web.

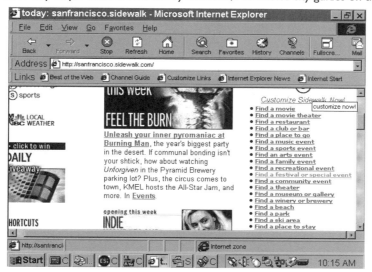

that would be of most help. The more you know about your customer pro-files, the better you'll know where to look. Remember, you are not doing pure research, you are looking for opinions, and newsgroups are the place to find them.

Structure your newsgroup search by thinking through your objectives and clarifying your own understanding about the product. For example:

- **Who uses this product?** If you manufacture suitcases, then groups related to travel might be a logical starting point

- **What do customers do with this product?** Your new product might be a small rolling case that can be used as a briefcase, legal case, or overnight travel case. Groups dealing with business travel as well as attorneys and their assistants might help you hit the mark. How about people complaining about airline restrictions on luggage size?

You might want to host a discussion group for your customers. They can post their observations and questions, and you can offer answers, assistance, and get some valuable information in the process.

Another tool at your disposal is an online survey. This can be done in the form of an e-mail request or an online meeting/interview. The response rate is usually higher for an e-mail request, especially if the survey consists primarily of checkboxes as opposed to fill-in-the-blank boxes.

## "Send This Supplier an E-Mail. What's Its Address?"

For the sake of practicality, use the phone. I know calling your suppliers seems archaic in this world of high-tech searchable resources, but it's probably the fastest route to get your answer. If, however, this is a supplier you haven't dealt with for a while and its information has been purged from your system, you'll have to start from scratch.

Help is on the way in the form of searchable directories on the Internet. (Refer to Chapter 3 for a discussion of different types of online directories.) Directories get their information from businesses and individuals that register with them, as well as mailing lists, USENET newsgroups, and web pages. The problem is that there are literally millions of people using the Internet, so the more you know about the person you are trying to find, the better. Remember, you may have to try more than one directory to hit your target.

Try searching for yourself first. If you or your company don't show up, you aren't in that directory. The best way to get listed is to register, which is as easy as looking for a link on the website labeled Register or List Your URL and then following the instructions, filling out an online form, and then submitting it. Once you are registered others can find you. If, however, you prefer to remain anonymous, then don't register in any online directory.

In addition to the directories discussed in Chapter 3, here are additional resources you might find useful:

- Searching Switchboard (**www.switchboard.com**) produces both e-mail addresses and "white pages" listings at the same time (see Figure 7-24).

- Big Yellow (**www.bigyellow.com**) is another very useful electronic phone directory for finding millions of business listings (see Figure 7-25).

- Company directories such as Hoover's Online (**www.hoovers.com**) might also be helpful. This is the electronic equivalent of the well-known paper business directory, Hoover's Handbook.

- Dun & Bradstreet (**www.dnb.com**) would be a resource you might have called in the past. Now you can have an online subscription and access to D&B business background reports.

Since AltaVista's database has more of a business orientation than other search engines, you might be able to search there using a product name to form a keyword search. That search should take you to the supplier information you need. If you are searching for an individual, type their name in the keyword search box encased in quotation marks. No luck? Try the Advanced search feature and type:

> **firstname NEAR lastname**

**Figure 7-24.** One way to track down John Doe's e-mail address is to do a search at Switchboard.

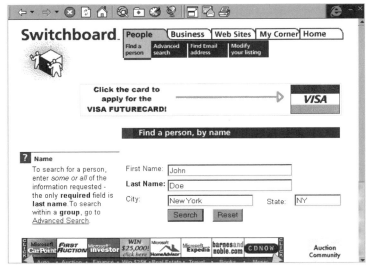

Reprinted with permission of Switchboard Incorporated.

**Figure 7-25.** Big Yellow locates businesses, people, and e-mail addresses and even industry-specific websites.

Reprinted with permission of Bell Atlantic.

## "Get a Copy of the Newest Software Upgrade for . . ."

Before I give you any references, let's be very clear. You never, ever, download software onto a company-owned computer without the express permission of the system administrator. Say it with me now . . . all together. We don't want to drive your corporate software folks into a nervous breakdown, and loading software without their knowledge will push them over the edge for sure.

Now that we are certain you or your boss wants to load this software onto a "safe" machine, here's where you can look.

Versions (**www.versions.com**) is a website where you can search by product for the latest versions of your software (see Figure 7-26). The majority of vendors are listed there with links to their sites and to the specific files you need. A subscription service is also offered that will notify you when software you are interested in is being upgraded. This is another example of "push" technology.

If you know the vendor's website address, you can go there directly without passing go or collecting $200. Some vendors have put direct links to their websites into the drop-down help menus of their software products. So you are in effect a click away from your software vendor. Selecting the web option from the drop-down help menu engages your browser, fills in the web page address embedded in the hyperlink, and away you go.

Don't forget about your hardware vendors. Hewlett-Packard (HP) is constantly updating the drivers for its line of printers, and they are available free for the asking. WinShareware (**www.winshareware.com**) has links to most vendors' sites so you can download software drivers, printer drivers, and other updates (see Figure 7-27). WinShareware also includes contact information for the technical assistance department of each company listed at the website.

There are different categories of software that are made available for download:

- **Freeware** is just that—free. There is no fee charged for its use.

- **Shareware** works on the honor system. It is available for download, and you are welcome to try it out. The author of the software will ask you to pay a registration fee if you intend to keep and use the product.

**Figure 7-26.** Versions offers a push service to alert you whenever there is an upgrade to a software package you use.

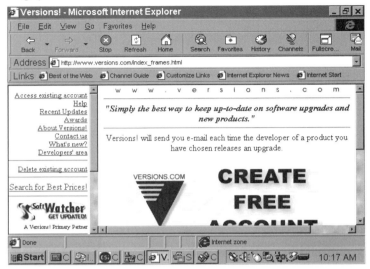

Reprinted with permission of Cirrus Arts Corporation.

**Figure 7-27.** WinShareware is a useful site for downloading driver software for your PC-compatible printer or other hardware peripherals.

Reprinted with permission of Hy Dencity Co.

- **Demoware** refers to a software program that is limited in some way. The vendor may have limited the features you can use; only after you pay for the program will the other features be unlocked. Or the vendor may limit the capacity of the program so that while you can try out all the features of a piece of planning software, for example, you can only put in thirty entries. Time limits are another way to encourage payment for the full-blown product. When you install the program, the clock starts ticking, and at the end of a thirty-day trial period the software will no longer work unless you purchase it.

This is probably about the time you'll start thinking, "If I can do all this on the Internet, I'll never talk to another living being again!" Depending on your personal philosophy, this could be good news or bad news, but the bottom line is that it's not true news.

If using the Net saves me from ever again hearing the phrase, "If you want to speak to a customer service representative, please press seven on your touch-tone phone now," then I'm thrilled. In reality, the recording should say, "Even though there's absolutely no hope of your ever speaking with a customer service representative, please feel free to sit back, relax, and push seven on your touch-tone phone now while you grow old with us listening to music on hold." I've been left on hold so long I was startled by the voice in my ear when someone finally did come on the line, and I had long forgotten what I was calling about in the first place.

I truly believe there are no customer service representatives; it is all a façade. Just like the one fruitcake that circles the globe during the holiday season. Be that as it may, I don't like to wait for anything or anybody.

Information online is instantly available, just waiting for you and me to access it. What this means is that when you do interact with people, you add value. You've got the edge because you already have the information. And the service representatives or other company contacts benefit when you make their jobs easier by working smart on your own.

# Conclusion

Picture this: It's Monday morning. You arrive at the office well rested from your weekend off, planning for the day at hand. You sit down at your desk, ready to begin a well-organized, productive, nonchaotic day. When the boss delivers the first barrage of requests for the day, you sit back, relax, smile, and think to yourself, "I'll just have my assistant take care of that."

The main purpose of this book was to get you thinking about how you can make the Internet work for you to save time and effort. I hope that as you have been reading each chapter, you have thought of even more ways that the Internet can assist you.

The Internet is an amazing resource that grows more valuable every day, and, if you use it to your advantage, so will you.

# Glossary

**acronym**   A word formed from the initial letters of each of the major parts of a compound term. An acronym appears as all capital letters.

**address**   The location of a site on the World Wide Web.

**analog line**   A communications pathway on which information is transmitted in analog form, which uses variable signals and electrical frequencies in transmitting information.

**bookmark**   A favorite website saved in a file so that the browser automatically goes to that site.

**Boolean**   A common system of logic that uses operators such as AND, OR, NOR, and NOT to find information with search engines.

**Boolean search**   A search query that uses Boolean operators.

**browser**   A program that displays and navigates web pages (see web browser).

**browsing**   Viewing and navigating web pages on the Internet.

**chat**   A typed conversation among computer users (see IRC).

**cyberspace**   The Internet.

**database**    A collection of related information in an easily accessible format, such as a table, form, or report. Databases can be used to sort, compare, and manipulate data in many other ways.

**directory**    A simulated file drawer. Web directories attempt to organize the Internet by subject. When using a directory, you are searching their topic lists much the same way you use an encyclopedia.

**domain name**    The name of a computer or collection of computers connected to the Internet. On the Internet, domain names typically end with a suffix denoting the type of site (e.g., microsoft.com). The ".com" in this case stands for a commercial company; ".edu" (educational institution) and ".gov" (government) are other common domain name extensions.

**download**    To receive a file sent from another computer via modem.

**e-mail**    Electronic mail.

**encryption**    The method of scrambling a message before delivery.

**FAQ**    A list of frequently asked questions and their answers related to a particular topic.

**filtering rules**    Instructions you establish to automatically delete, file, or otherwise act upon electronic messages.

**FTP**    File Transfer Protocol. A standard protocol that allows files to be copied from one computer to another.

**flame**    An inflammatory remark used in an electronic message.

**freeware**    Software that is distributed without charge on the Internet.

**gopher**    A nested menu system used to organize and display text files stored within data libraries.

**home page**    The name for the main page in a website; the first page encountered for a given site.

**HTML**    Hypertext Markup Language. Programming language used to create web pages that contain connections called hyperlinks.

**HTTP**    Hypertext Transfer Protocol. The set of standards that let users of the World Wide Web exchange information found in web pages.

**hyperlink**    An icon, graphic, or word in a file that, when clicked with the mouse, automatically opens another file for viewing. Hyperlinks include the address or names of the files to which they point, but typically this code is hidden from the user.

**Internet**    A global Transmission Control Protocol/Internet Protocol (TCP/IP) network linking millions of computers for communications purposes. Also known as cyberspace, the Net, and the Web. A network of computers linked together to allow information sharing.

**IP address**    A numeric representation of a computer's location within a network. IP addresses are written as four groups of numbers (each group may consist of as many as three numbers separated by periods. An example of an IP address is 203.176.56.193.

**IRC**    Internet Relay Chat. A type of interactive communication on the Internet in which computer users engage in real-time communication. Joining an IRC discussion requires a connection to the Internet and IRC client software.

**ISDN**    Integrated Services Digital Network. A digital telecommunications network that can transmit data at 128 kilobytes per second. Special equipment is required to connect to ISDN lines.

**ISP**    Internet Service Provider. A company that provides software and access to the Internet.

**modem**   Modulator/demodulator. A device that lets a computer transmit and receive digital information (i.e., the 1s and 0s of computer communications) over analog telephone lines.

**netiquette**   Etiquette on the Net.

**newsgroup**   A virtual area on the Internet reserved for the posting of messages to discuss a certain topic.

**online**   Being on the Web. The opposite of "offline," which is when you are not connected.

**page**   A part of a website; same as web page.

**push technology**   Technology that "pushes" information from a website to a user's computer, according to the user's individual preferences, instead of the user having to go out and find it through a web search. You must subscribe to these services.

**search engine**   Software that searches through a database. Users type a keyword query (i.e., descriptor words), and the search engine responds with a list of all sites in its database fitting the query description.

**shareware**   Software distributed on the Internet that may require a nominal fee for its use.

**spiders**   Programs that automatically search the Web, compiling information on websites and the information they contain. Also called robots, web crawlers, or worms.

**surfing**   Same as browsing the Web.

**TCP/IP**   Transmission Control Protocol/Internet Protocol. A protocol governing communication among all computers on the Internet. It dictates how packets of information are sent over the networks and ensures the reliability of data transmission.

**URL**   Uniform or Universal Resource Locator. A standardized naming or addressing system for documents and media accessible over the Internet.

**USENET**   A giant bulletin board on the Internet consisting of newsgroups and discussion groups.

**Web**   Short for the World Wide Web.

**web browser**   Software that gives access to and navigation of the World Wide Web using a graphical interface that lets users click buttons, icons, and menu options.

**web page**   A document written in HTML that can be accessed on the Internet.

**web server**   The computer that processes World Wide Web accesses for a given site.

**website**   A group of files that are housed at a single domain address and provide information such as text, graphics, and audio to users as well as connections (called hypertext links or links) to other websites on the Internet. Every website has a home page, the initial document seen by users, which acts as a table of contents to other available web pages and offerings at the site.

**webmaster**   The person who develops and maintains a particular website.

**World Wide Web (WWW)**   Also simply referred to as the Web. A graphical interface for the Internet that is composed of hyperlinks. These links are graphics or different-colored text that contain programming instructions that provide the connection to the next site.

**zine**   An online magazine.

# Useful Websites

## Airline Reservations

American Airlines ...............................**www.americanair.com**

British Airways...................................**www.british-airways.com**

Continental .......................................**www.flycontinental.com**

Delta ................................................**www.delta-air.com**

Japan Airlines ...................................**www.jal.co.jp**

KLM Royal Dutch ...............................**www.klm.nl**

Northwest ..........................................**www.nwa.com**

Qantas ..............................................**www.qantas.com.au**

Scandinavian ....................................**www.sas.se**

TWA .................................................**www.twa.com**

USAir................................................**www.usair.com**

United ...............................................**www.ual.com**

## *Business and Law*

Collier and Associates Law Firm  ........**www.collierlaw.com/**

Department of Labor............................**www.dol.gov/**

Consumer Reports Online  .................**www.comsumerreports.org**

## *Car Rentals*

Alamo  .................................................**www.goalamo.com**

Avis .....................................................**www.avis.com**

Hertz ...................................................**www.hertz.com**

National................................................**www.nationalcar.com**

## *Financial and Business Resources*

American Express................................**www.americanexpress.com**

Barron's................................................**www.enews.com/magazines/barrons/**

BusinessWeek  ....................................**www.businessweek.com**

Dow Jones  ..........................................**bis.dowjones.com**

Dreyfus Information..............................**www.dreyfus.com/funds**

Dun & Bradstreet  ................................**www.dnb.com**

Fastest Free Quotes,
Thomson Real-Time Quotes................**www.thomsontq.com**

Fidelity Investments ...........................**www.fid.com**

Fraud Information ..............................**www.fraud.org**

Internet Business Directory ...............**www.ibi.com/search.htm**

Janus Funds .......................................**www.networth.galt.com/janus**

Morningstar.........................................**www.morningstar.net**

My Yahoo Ticker .................................**my.yahoo.co/ticker.html**

Nasdaq ...............................................**www.nasdaq.com/**

NY Stock Exchange ...........................**www.nyse.com**

Nikkei Net ...........................................**www.nikkei.co.jp/enews/**

Prudential Securities..........................**www.prusec.com**

Stocks & Bonds..................................**www.secapl.com**


## *General Business Information*

Business Equipment ..........................**www.buyerszone.com/index.html**

European Business Information .........**www.euroseek.net**

Global Directory .................................**www.555-1212.com/**

Mobilesoft ..........................................**www.mobilesoft.com**

Presenters University ........................**www.presentationuniversity.com**

Print Media Online .............................**www.owt.com/dircon**

So Many Sites Resource ...................**www.pcworld.com/theweb**

## Government

Census Bureau ......................................**www.census.gov**

Center for Disease Control ..................**www.cdc.gov/**

CIA Server ..........................................**www.odci.gov/cia**

Federal Government
   Agency Directory ............................**www.lib.lsu.edu/gov/fedgov.html**

Fed World ...........................................**www.fedworld.gov**

IRS .....................................................**www.irs.ustreas.gov/**

Library of Congress ...........................**www.loc.gov**

Supreme Court Decisions...................**www.law.cornell.edu/supct/**

Supreme Court Justices .....................**www.gov.mci.net/fed/jud/jud.html**

United Nations ...................................**www.un.org**

U.S. Consulate Addresses .................**www.immigration.com/
us_consulates.html**

White House .......................................**www.whitehouse.gov/**

## Hotel Reservations

Crowne Plaza Hotels ..........................**www.crowneplaza.com**

Days Inn ..............................................**www.daysinn.com/daysinn.html**

Doubletree Guest Suites.....................**www.doubletreehotels.com**

Embassy Suites ..................................**www.embassy-suites.com**

Marriott, Residence Inn.......................**www.marriott.com**

Four Seasons ....................................**www.fshr.com**

Hampton Inns ...................................**www.hampton-inn.com**

Harley Hotels ...................................**www.harleyhotels.com**

Hilton Hotels ....................................**www.hilton.com**

Holiday Inn ......................................**www.holiday-inn.com**

Homewood Suites.............................**www.homewood-suites.com**

Hyatt, Red Lion, Renaissance,
Sonesta, Wyndham............................**www.travelweb.com**

Intercontinental Hotels .......................**www.interconti.com**

Radisson ..........................................**www.radisson.com**

Ramada  ..........................................**www.ramada.com/ramada.html**

Sheraton ..........................................**www.sheraton.com**

Super 8 Motels .................................**www.super8motels.com/super8.html**

Westin Hotels ...................................**www.westin.com**

## *International Travel Guides (see also Travel)*

Arthur Frommer's Outspoken
Encyclopedia of Travel .......................**www.frommers.com**

Fodor's Travel Service
Personal Trip Planner ........................... **www.fodors.com**

Worldview Systems.............................. **www.wvs.com**

## News

C-Span ................................................ **www.c-span.org/**

CNN Interactive.................................... **www.cnn.com**

Electronic Telegraph ........................... **www.telegraph.co.uk**

The Gate ............................................. **www.sfgate.com**

Nando Times........................................ **www.nando.net**

NewsLink.............................................. **www.newslink.org**

The New York Times ........................... **www.nytimes.com**

Reuters ............................................... **www.yahoo.com/headline/current/news**

USA Today ........................................ **www.usatoday.com**

Wall Street Journal Money &
Investment Update ............................ **www.update.wsj.com**

Weather............................................... **www.clunix.cl.msu.edu/weather**

## Online Technical Support

Cartridges USA.................................... **www.cartridgesusa.com/related.html**

C/NET ................................................. **www.cnet.com/Resources**

Fix It Now ................................................ **www.zdnet.com/zdhelp/**
**fixit_help/fixit_help.html**

HelpMeNow .......................................... **www.helpmenow.com**

Modemhelp .......................................... **www.modemhelp.com**

Mr. Fixit ............................................... **www.needservice.com/mrfixit.htm**

PC Guide ............................................. **www.pcguide.com**

PC Lube & Tune ................................... **pclt.cis.yale.edu/pclt/default.htm**

PC Mechanic........................................ **pcmech.pair.com**

PC Video Hardware FAQ .................... **www.heartlab.rri.uwo.ca/vidafaq.html**

Printer & Photocopier
Troubleshooting & Repair ................... **www.paranoia.com/~filipg/**
**HTML/REPAIR/F_Printer.html**

Tech Net .............................................. **www.leadingedge.com/frmain.htm**

Techni-Help ......................................... **www.freepchelp.com**

USA Today Answer Desk ................... **ww.usatoday.com/life/cyber/bonus/qa**

## Reference Sites

Bartlett's Familiar Quotations ............. **www.columbia.edu/acis/**
**bartleby/bartlett**

Better Business Bureau ...................... **www.bbb.org/**

@Brint: A Business
Researcher's Interests ....................... **www.brint.com/interest.html**

Big Book ..............................................**www.bigbook.com**

Library of Congress ...........................**lcweb.loc.gov/**

OneLook Dictionaries ........................**www.onelook.com**

U.S. Census Bureau ...........................**www.census.gov/**

## *Restaurants*

Cuisinenet ...........................................**www.cuisinenet.com**

Fodor's Restaurant Index ...................**www.fodors.com/ri.cgi**

Microsoft's Sidewalk ...........................**www.sidewalk.com**

## *Shipping*

DHL.....................................................**www.dhl.com**

Federal Express ..................................**www.fedex.com**

FedEx Airbill Tracking Form ...............**www.fedex.com/us/tracking/**

UPS.....................................................**www.ups.com**

United States Postal Service .............**www.usps.gov**

## *Travel*

BizTravel .............................................**www.biztravel.com**

Centers for Disease Control ...............**www.cdc.gov/travel**

Expedia ..............................................**www.expedia.com**

Fodor's ...............................................**www.fodors.com**

Frequent flyer programs .....................**www.theffpsite.org**

General travel information...................**www.priceline.comn**

The Trip ..............................................**www.thetrip.com**

Travelocity ..........................................**www.travelocity.com**

The Weather Channel.........................**www.weather.com/twc/homepage.twc**

# Recommended Reading

If you liked *CyberAssistant* check out these career-building books from AMACOM

## CyberMeeting
### How to Link People and Technology in Your Organization
*James L. Creighton and James W.R. Adams*
This breakthrough book looks at how cutting edge computer technologies are transforming our concept of what "meeting" is—and helps companies avoid the millions of dollars that can be wasted when new "collaborative technology" is introduced.
**$27.95  Order #0352-XCYB**          **ISBN-8144-0352-2**

## CyberWriting
### How to Promote Your Product or Service Online (without being flamed)
*Joe Vitale*
The online world is heavily dependent on good writing—and the more powerful your writing skills, the better change you have for business success in cyberspace. *CyberWriting* provides you with exactly what you need to create highly targeted copy that's geared to online conventions, technology, and culture.
**$18.95  Order #7918-XCYB**          **ISBN-8144-7918-9**

## The Smart Way to Buy Information Technology
### How to Maximize Value and Avoid Costly Pitfalls
*Brad L. Peterson and Diane M. Carco*
*The Smart Way to Buy Information Technology* is the cheat sheet you need to put you in the driver's seat. In a clear, common-sense manner, Smart Way reveals the ploys of vendors and how CIO's can counteract them."—*CIO Magazine*
**$35.00  Order #0387-XCYB**              **ISBN 0-8144-0387-5**

## The Internet Glossary and Quick Reference Guide
*Alan Freedman, Alfred Glossbrenner, and Emily Glossbrenner*
This internet travel guide will make any "cyber journey" smoother and more productive. Packed with up-to-the-minute definitions and crystal-clear explanations, anyone venturing into cyberspace will find this Internet reference as essential as their on-line browser.
**$24.95  Order #7979-XCYB**              **ISBN 0-8144-7979-0**

## The Computer Desktop Encyclopedia, Second Edition
*Alan Freedman*
The most comprehensive computer reference available! More than 10,000 definitions and explanations, including 5,000 new or revised terms. Covers every topic imaginable—from laptop to mainframe microchip to the World Wide Web. Ideal for beginners, power users, or computer professionals. Free CD-ROM for Windows version included inside.
**$45.00  Order #7985-XCYB**              **ISBN 0-8144-7985-5**

## e-shock: The Electronic Shopping Revolution
### Strategies for Retailers and Manufacturers
*Michael de Kare-Silver*

"Read this book to learn how today's companies are exploiting electronic commerce and radically altering the buying and selling landscape. Michael de Kare-Silver excellently describes the golden opportunities emerging in the marketplace. I read it through without stopping and wished there was more. This book will help you answer whether your company is ready for virtual selling and how to proceed."—Philip Kotler, Distinguished Professor of International Marketing, J.L. Kellogg Graduate School of Management, Northwestern University.

**$29.95  Order #0497-XCYB**                **ISBN 0-8144-0497-9**

## Public Relations on the Net
### Winning Strategies to Inform and Influence the Media, the Investment Community, the Government, the Public, and More!
*Shel Holtz*

This guide explains how to conduct effective and measurable P.R. on the Net. Rich in step-by-step instructions and action plans, it's also studded with instructive examples of companies that leverage the Internet and World Wide Web to improve relationships with journalists, investors, civic groups, and other constituents.

**$24.95  Order #7987-XCYB**                **ISBN 0-8144-7987-1**

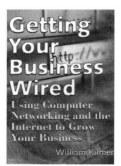

## Getting Your Business Wired
### Using Computer Networking and the Internet to Grow Your Business
*William E. Kilmer*

*Getting Your Business Wired* makes it easy for any type of enterprise to set up an effective computer network. Readers who follow its detailed, user-friendly guidance may expect significant increases in savings, productivity, and profits— and reap the benefits of a new level of competitiveness. Everything you need to know about available technologies and applications, sources of equipment and services, advice on taming the Internet, and step-by-step guidance to planning, budgeting , and managing a computer network.

**$24.95  Order #7007-XCYB**                **ISBN 0-8144-7007-6**

# Index